# THE BECOMING
## THE RIPPLE WORKBOOK

YOUR GUIDE TO
EXPONENTIALLY
INCREASING YOUR
PROFESSIONAL
SUCCESS AND
INFLUENCE

DAPHNE VALCIN

I dedicate this workbook to all of those who have continuously become the ripple in the lives of those around them in truly positive ways. These beacons of light are people like Vallay Varro, Stephanie Whitehead, Citra Registe Joseph, Laura Knights, Tammy Way, and countless other colleagues, leaders, mentors, and teachers who have been a guiding light and inspiration to so many, including me. I thank you.

THIS BOOK BELONGS TO

_____

# CONTENTS

## PART 4: YOUR ENVIRONMENT

## PART 5: YOUR SPECIAL TOUCH

# INTRODUCTION

This workbook was created as a companion to my book, "Becoming the Ripple: Your Guide To Exponentially Increasing Your Professional Success and Influence" a book written as a result of my working with over 400 individual clients and over 200 organizational clients for more than ten years through coaching, consulting, training, and program development and witnessing what causes the most tremendous success in individuals and companies, and what can hinder progress.

The Becoming the Ripple title came from my observation of the ripple effect that happens when people operate entirely within their potential, exceeding expectations, feeling fully aligned with their work, and pushing past challenges. This ripple effect includes teams, companies, and even the personal lives of those individuals being impacted. When individuals create this ripple effect in a way that is sustained over time, they are continuously creating the ripple–in essence, they are "becoming the ripple." They are regularly exploring how they can grow and how they can impact those around them, even as their priorities, roles, or capacity change. I hope this workbook supports you practically and inspires you to shift in ways beyond what you can even imagine.

In the following pages, I'll use my signature WAVES™ framework for how to grow your influence and impact to expound on what it can look like for you to be "becoming the ripple," both personally and professionally.

- Part 1 of this workbook will help you expound on your **Why** for pursuing your vision and goals.
- Part 2 explores how you can expand your impact through consistent, strategic **Action**.
- Part 3 equips you with tools to exude more of what you desire to be perceived as through your **Voice**.
- Part 4 will guide you towards having a more noticeable impact on your work **Environment** that might result in greater opportunities.
- Part 5–quite possibly my favorite part–is about clarifying your **Special Touch** in order to use your unique values and strengths**.**

**How should you use the workbook?** This workbook consists of 15 chapters. My recommendation is that you schedule time on a weekly basis to delve into each chapter of this workbook, so that by the end of 15 weeks, you will have taken consistent action towards increasing your influence, impact, and life trajectory through the exercises and reflections in this workbook. As an alternative, you can complete the exercises in this workbook little by little, working on one chapter per day or even per month, or at another pace that suits your schedule best. There are exercises for reflection, sections of the workbook where you'll be creating action plans, and even spaces set aside to track the progress that will be associated with your growth and development. I would also suggest utilizing an accountability partner or even an accountability group to share your plans and progress with as you move through the workbook for an additional layer of accountability. And at the end of each chapter, you'll have a dedicated space to reflect on your most significant takeaways, reflections, or insights as you move forward.

The exercises in this workbook have literally transformed the lives of professionals around the world. My hope is that this workbook and all that is within it will do the same for you.

# PART ONE
# YOUR WHY

# CHAPTER ONE

# Your "Why" Will Push You Further Faster

*"It's not the will to win that matters—everyone has that. It's the will to prepare to win that matters."*

**—PAUL BRYANT**

How would you feel if you knew without a shadow of a doubt that every action you took professionally was grounded in your purpose and interests? Exploring your greatest motivations for career advancement can open the door for you to be more aligned with what you truly desire from your work, desired promotions, and work culture. When you're more aligned, you're better positioned to create a ripple of impact for those around you. Complete the following "The Core of Your Why" activity to explore some core motivations for your desire for career advancement.

## The Core of Your Why

Below, you will list 5 core reasons for your motivation for career advancement. For each of the 5 core reasons associated with your "why" below, you'll explore why that core reason is important to you. Then, you'll dig deeper and further explore what led you to share why your core reason was so important to you. This activity will reveal some of the most foundational reasons why you are pursuing your career advancement goals.

## Core of Your Why #1

| 1. What is 1 core reason for your motivation for career advancement? | 2. Why is that core reason important to you? | 3. Why is what you said in your previous answer important to you? |
|---|---|---|
| *Example: One core reason for my motivation for career advancement is making my mother proud, who contributed a lot of time and effort into who I am today.* | *Example: That core reason is important to me because I want to be someone who contributes to others' success just as my mother has done.* | *Example: What I said in my previous answer is important to me because I believe that we are all meant to live in our purpose and help others to live in their purpose as well.* |

## Core of Your Why #2

| 1. What is 1 core reason for your motivation for career advancement? | 2. Why is that core reason important to you? | 3. Why is what you said in your previous answer important to you? |
|---|---|---|
|  |  |  |

## Core of Your Why #3

| 1. What is 1 core reason for your motivation for career advancement? | 2. Why is that core reason important to you? | 3. Why is what you said in your previous answer important to you? |
| --- | --- | --- |
| | | |

## Core of Your Why #4

| 1. What is 1 core reason for your motivation for career advancement? | 2. Why is that core reason important to you? | 3. Why is what you said in your previous answer important to you? |
| --- | --- | --- |
| | | |

| 1. What is 1 core reason for your motivation for career advancement? | 2. Why is that core reason important to you? | 3. Why is what you said in your previous answer important to you? |
|---|---|---|
| | | |

## Career Motivation Ranking

Below, you'll see a list of common motivators for career advancement. Choose your top 5 motivators from the list below.

**Community:** You love the feeling of community you get at work, and doing great work makes you feel like you're contributing significantly to your colleagues.

**Financial Freedom:** The desire to have wealth and disposable income to spend on whatever you would like.

**Honoring a Loved One:** You do the work you do and maybe even do it in a certain way in honor of a mentor, family member, or someone else who had a significant impact on you. That person directly or indirectly inspired you to do great work for several reasons. They may have also helped you expand your vision of the success you could have through your work.

**Legacy Building:** You want your children and your children's children to have the financial success, degrees, or experiences you have had.

**Mentorship:** Your desire to operate with excellence or get promoted comes from you wanting to be an example for other colleagues you wish to serve as an example for.

**Peace:** You feel like success brings you more peace through the experiences, living situation, or financial success you have, so you put forth quite a bit of effort in what you do in order to have more of that peace.

**Spirituality:** You are driven intensely by the spiritual or religious practices you follow that cause you to put forth great effort in what you do and how you do it.

**Time Freedom:** You know that a particular kind of income or a certain kind of work in a specific role gives you the flexibility to do what you'd like when you'd like to do it, whether that means spending more time with family or having more time to relax.

**Other**

Now, rank your top 5 motivators in order from the motivators that are most important to you to the 1 that is least important.

1) _____
2) _____
3) _____
4) _____
5) _____

Reflect and Write: Why are these top motivators important to you?

_____

_____

_____

_____

_____

_____

_____

_____

Reflect and Write: How do your greatest motivators for career advancement impact what kind of career path you will take?

_____

_____

_____

_____

_____

_____

_____

_____

## Career Visioning

Your vision for the future can be what allows you to move steadily towards the right destination and impact, even when challenges come up along the way. What are 3 key aspects of what you want your career to look like **1 year from now** when it comes to opportunities, your values, work culture, location, type of work, professional development, your strengths, your areas for growth, or anything else that is important to you?

*Example:*
*1) I have been promoted to at least one level beyond where I currently am.*
*2) I have learned how to manage up by ensuring I ask at least one question or propose one solution during my 1:1s with my manager.*
*3) I have attained a project management certification.*

1) _____

2) _____

3) _____

What are 3 key aspects of what you want your career to look like **5 years from now** when it comes to opportunities, your values, work culture, location, type of work, professional development, your strengths, your areas for growth, or anything else that is important to you?

*Example:*
*1) I have increased my salary by $20,000.*
*2) I have joined a public speaking professional development organization.*
*3) I have attained a Lean Six Sigma certification.*

1) _____

2) _____

3) _____

What are 3 key aspects of what I want your career to look like **ten years from now** when it comes to opportunities, your values, work culture, location, type of work, professional development, your strengths, your areas for growth, or anything else that is important to you?

*Example:*
*1) I have increased my salary by $50,000.*
*2) I have joined a professional association for IT professionals.*
*3) I have moved to one of the major cities where the company I work for has a headquarters to have more future career advancement opportunities.*

1) _____

2) _____

3) _____

## From Ripples to Waves: Sustaining forward movement

**Make reflecting on your "why" a habit.** Consider adding a reminder to your calendar, on a weekly, monthly, or quarterly basis, to revisit what you've identified as your biggest "why" for your approach to your career advancement.

Your why will push you
further, *faster*.

# Reflections

# CHAPTER 2

# Put Your Why in Front of You

*"If you change the way you look at things, the things you look at change."*

**—WAYNE DYER**

Those who have created some of the greatest ripples of impact have strived to clarify their greatest motivations in different seasons of their lives, personally or professionally. Periodically exploring those greatest motivations more deeply allows us to be continuously "becoming the ripple" for ourselves and those around us. Have you ever heard the phrase, "Out of sight. Out of mind." When we don't take time to reflect on what's important, we can easily lose sight of that. The consequences of that can be misalignment, heading in a direction we actually don't want to go, feeling stuck, or feeling unmotivated. Regularly reminding ourselves of what our "why" is can help us to stay focused on what's most important, fueling our ability to increase our influence and impact where it matters most.

## Visualizing Your Motivations

For each of your top 5 greatest motivations, list 3 prospective physical items or digital images that might immediately remind you of each in order to put your "why" in front of you.

| Top Motivators | Physical or Digital Items to Immediately Remind You of Each |
|---|---|
| *Example:*<br>*Legacy Building* | *Example:*<br>*1. Photo of my family around my desk.*<br>*2. A daily calendar reminder that pops up on my phone to remind me of my why each morning.*<br>*3. A candle made by my daughters on my desk.* |
| **1.** | **1.**<br><br>**2.**<br><br>**3.** |
| **2.** | **1.**<br><br>**2.**<br><br>**3.** |
| **3.** | **1.**<br><br>**2.**<br><br>**3.** |
| **4.** | **1.**<br><br>**2.**<br><br>**3.** |

| | |
|---|---|
| **5.** | **1.**<br><br>**2.**<br><br>**3.** |

Now choose your top 5 physical or digital items that can remind you of your motivators. Choose where you might place some or all of these items as visual reminders of your motivators. Prospective locations for these items to be placed include around your home, on your wall, on your desk, in your car, on the lock screen of your phone, as wallpaper on your laptop, in a physical or digital folder, or somewhere else you feel would work well.

*Example:*
*Physical or Digital Item)* <u>A candle made by my daughters</u> *Location:* <u>On my desk</u> .

Physical or Digital Item #1) _____ Location: _____

Physical or Digital Item #2) _____ Location: _____

Physical or Digital Item #3) _____ Location: _____

Physical or Digital Item #4) _____ Location: _____

Physical or Digital Item #5) _____ Location: _____

## Digital or Physical Vision Board Creation

A vision board is a physical embodiment of some of your most prominent goals, objectives, and dreams for your future. Creating a vision board for your personal and professional success is a tangible way to have your greatest motivations in front of you. You can also regularly reference your vision board to track your progress toward your goals.

Some people have vision boards that are more short-term focused with items that represent what they hope to work towards in the year ahead.

Others have vision boards with a longer-term focus. In this case, the vision board may represent goals, objectives, and dreams that might be desired in the next 5, 10, 20, or more years, for example.

Creating a vision board can

## Action steps for creating a physical vision board:

**Materials Needed:**

- One sheet of paper or poster board (choose from A3 size: 11.7 x 16.5 inches, A4 size: 8.3 x 11.7 inches, or letter size: 8.5 x 11 inches)
- 5 to 10 magazines (ideally ones that include visuals or text related to topics like lifestyle, career, health, travel, or inspiration)
- Scissors
- Glue stick or liquid glue
- Optional: markers, stickers, or other decorative supplies

**Instructions:**

- **Reflect on Your Motivations:** Take a few minutes to think about your biggest motivations in life. Some examples of this are family, faith, health, freedom, success, creativity, purpose, or impact. Write down 3–5 of your top motivators.
- **Browse and Collect:** Flip through the magazines and look for images, words, or phrases that align with your top motivations. Don't overthink it. Cut out anything that inspires you or represents what you want more of in your life.
- **Gather Enough Visuals:** Aim to collect enough images, words, or phrases to fill your sheet of paper or board without overcrowding visually.
- **Arrange Before You Glue:** Lay out the pieces you have cut out from the magazine on your sheet of paper without gluing them yet. Move them around until you're happy with the overall look and message. Consider grouping items by theme or motivation if that helps you visualize everything on your paper more clearly.
- **Glue It Down:** Once you're satisfied with your layout, use your glue stick or liquid glue to attach each piece to the paper. Press firmly so everything sticks well to your sheet of paper.
- **Add Additional Pieces (Optional):** If you'd like, you can use markers, stickers, tape, shiny paper, glitter, or other tools to decorate your vision board.
- **Display Your Vision Board:** Place your finished vision board somewhere you'll see it often. This could be on your wall, your desk, your closet door, or even inside a binder or journal cover.

## Action steps for creating a digital vision board:

- **Choose a Design Platform:** Use an online design tool like Canva or another platform you're comfortable with to create your digital vision board.
- **Set Up Your Document:** Start a new project and choose a size that works for you. Some common options for vision board sizes include A4 (8.3 x 11.7 inches), letter size (8.5 x 11 inches), or a custom size that fits your screen or intended use.

- **Add Inspiring Images:** Search for and insert images that represent your greatest motivations. You can use the image library within your design tool or upload images from other websites (making sure you have permission to use them if needed).
- **Include Meaningful Text:** Add words, affirmations, or short phrases that represent your core motivations. These might include goals, values, or quotes that inspire you.
- **Personalize and Arrange:** Move the images and text around until you feel your vision board is complete. Use colors, fonts, or backgrounds that resonate with you and enhance the overall message.
- **Save and Display:** Once complete, download your digital vision board. You can then save it to a location that's best for you to view it periodically. Some examples include saving it as your desktop wallpaper, phone background, or screensaver, or printing it out and placing it somewhere physically visible.

What kind of vision board might you create?

\_\_\_ A physical vision board
\_\_\_ A digital vision board

When will you create your vision board?

_____

Where will your vision board be located?

_____


Daily Reminders That Increase Self-Confidence

Sometimes, negative self-talk or external challenges can get in the way of remembering your "why" and increasing your self-confidence. It's almost as if negative self-talk either halts your ripple of impact or creates negative ripples of impact.

What might be 1 or more top approaches for you not to allow internal or external challenges to get in the way of your "why"?

**Reading relevant topics:** Whether it's an audiobook, physical book, blog posts, or some other kind of reading, reading can influence the self-talk you might be experiencing at work and allow you to be more aligned with the thoughts you would like to think about success, taking on more complex work, engaging successfully with direct reports, managing up, and more.

**Progress charts:** Create a visual that tracks your priorities, project targets, milestones, or strategic plan implementation progress regularly within your line of sight at work. As you progress, this tool can help you experience positive reinforcement towards the goals that matter most to you.

**Quotes or affirmations:** Quotes and affirmations, including excerpts from books that have inspired you or equipped you well, when placed around your workspace, can give you the jolt you need when you feel your work has become routine, when challenges come your way, or when new opportunities arise that you might not yet know how to navigate.

**Achievement reminders:** Diplomas, certificates, trophies, awards, and other symbols of your achievement can serve as reminders to build on your past successes and remind you to tap into more of your potential.

**Other:**

_____

_____

_____

_____

## From ripples to waves: Sustaining forward movement

**Regularly reflect on your "why".** Sometimes when we forget our why, life becomes routine, and we don't strive as much for what we are meant to do or who we are meant to be in the world. Daily, monthly, or quarterly, schedule reflecting on your "why" for a few seconds or even a few minutes. Think about the ripple that could be created in your life and the lives of others if you operate more and more in your "why". Reflect on what is aligned and not aligned with your greatest motivations, values, and dreams in your current life. Visualize and reflect on what it looks like to operate fully with your "why" in mind. What would you do differently? What would you be more of? What would you be less of? What would you do more of? What would you do less of?

Come away from that time of reflection with just 1 - 3 shifts that you'd like to make to operate more fully in your "why".

Be intentional.
What you reflect on most
becomes your greatest focus.

# Reflections

_____

_____

_____

_____

_____

_____

_____

_____

_____

_____

_____

_____

_____

_____

_____

_____

_____

_____

# CHAPTER 3
# Stay Ready

*"The pessimist sees difficulty in every opportunity. The optimist sees opportunity in every difficulty."*

**—WINSTON CHURCHILL**

Have you ever wondered why some people seem so disciplined? This most likely has very much to do with the valuable habits they've formed over time. Habits are formed through a series of cues, responses, and rewards. This chapter's title, "Stay Ready," relates to your understanding of what is causing you to do the things you do, whether those things benefit you or hinder you from doing the things that will bring you closer to the vision of who you desire to be. You'll learn how to "stay ready," being prepared to pursue your actions, habits, and routines successfully, as you are "becoming the ripple" in your professional and personal life.

## Habit Loops Old and New Exercise

The following process typically occurs before and during the implementation of a habit. This process is called a habit loop:

- **External cue:** A location may influence a specific behavior. This might be a location, event, sound, visual, or something else. For instance, I've noticed that when I work on my laptop from the kitchen, I tend to snack about twice as much as I do when I work from my office space, which is located away from the kitchen.

- **Internal cue:** A certain feeling might also result in a particular behavior taking place. This might include feeling tired, bored, angry, frustrated, or anxious, as well as experiencing muscle pain, hunger, a specific memory, or a behavioral cue like sitting down in one particular location. Feeling stressed, for example, might cause certain people to tap their pencils on a table, sigh, procrastinate, or bite their nails.
- **Response:** This is what happens as a result of the external or internal cue. Perhaps sitting down in a specific location in your home causes you to daydream while looking outside the window.
- **Reward:** This is the positive feeling that occurs as a result of the action. Eating a quick snack every time you walk into your kitchen might give you a sense of satisfaction, for example.

Below, you'll identify the cue, response, and reward that happen during a habit you would like to change, and then identify the cue, routine, and reward that might be associated with a new habit. You'll do this for 3 habits:

*Example:*
*Old Habit Loop 1:*

| CUE | I put down my bag on my chair after walking through my office door. |
|---|---|
| RESPONSE | I head towards the break room and chat casually with my co-workers for 20 - 25 minutes as I grab a cup of coffee. |
| REWARD | I feel more socially connected to my co-workers, but also end up losing time to be productive during an important part of my workday. |

*New Habit Loop 1:*

| CUE | I put down my bag on my chair after walking through my office door. |
|---|---|
| RESPONSE | Before going to the breakroom, I write down my top 3 priorities for the day in a Google Doc, block time to complete each priority, and complete one of those priorities before heading to the break room to grab a coffee and connect with my co-workers. |
| REWARD | I feel a sense of accomplishment and a greater sense of direction that can lend itself to my career advancement and optimization. I am also able to get a sense of connection with my co-workers at a more optimal time. |

## Old Habit Loop 1:

| CUE | |
|---|---|
| RESPONSE | |
| REWARD | |

## New Habit Loop 1:

| CUE | |
|---|---|
| RESPONSE | |
| REWARD | |

## Old Habit Loop 2:

| CUE | |
|---|---|
| RESPONSE | |
| REWARD | |

## New Habit Loop 2:

| CUE | |
|---|---|
| RESPONSE | |
| REWARD | |

**Old Habit Loop 3:**

| CUE | |
|---|---|
| RESPONSE | |
| REWARD | |

**New Habit Loop 3:**

| CUE | |
|---|---|
| RESPONSE | |
| REWARD | |

## Game-Changing Habit Tracking

There are so many habits we can develop that could truly impact our lives personally or professionally. All together, the positive habits we implement can create, *not just ripples,* but waves of impact in our lives and the lives of others. What are 3 habits that you could develop that are highly realistic for you to implement and that would immensely impact you or significantly impact the influence you have on others? Track your implementation of this new habit over a 7-day period to see if you can consecutively implement the new habit daily. Some examples of game-changing habits might be:

- Journaling
- Having a daily wrap-up and planning time
- Taking a daily walk
- Reaching out to connect with 1 colleague or mentor daily
- Coordinating or implementing action steps from meetings after each meeting
- Morning meditation or prayer
- Eating lunch without working
- Meal prep
- Morning affirmations
- Stopping by each direct report's office to check in and say hello each morning

If you worked on improving 3 game-changing habits at a time every 3 months, that would be 12 significant habits changed per year and 60 key habits changed every 5 years, with hundreds of habits you'd be using to enhance your quality of life, impact, and influence over your lifetime. The ripple you would create would eventually turn into waves of impact through your shift in habits.

What are the 3 game-changing habits that you would like to implement or improve daily?

*Example:*
*1. Meal prep for my lunch the next day daily*
*2. Eating lunch without working after reducing my time working during lunch gradually*
*3. Having a daily wrap-up and planning time*

1. _____

2. _____

3. _____

Below, track your ability to implement or improve each habit for 7 days:

**Habit 1:**

_____

**Date/ Timeframes Implemented or Improved:**

Day 1 _____

Day 2 _____

Day 3 _____

Day 4 _____

Day 5 _____

Day 6 _____

Day 7 _____

**Habit 2:**

_____

**Date/ Timeframes Implemented or Improved:**

Day 1 _____

Day 2 _____

Day 3 _____

Day 4 _____

Day 5 _____

Day 6 _____

Day 7 _____

**Habit 3:**

_____

**Date/ Timeframes Implemented or Improved:**

Day 1 _____

Day 2 _____

Day 3 _____

Day 4 _____

Day 5 _____

Day 6 _____

Day 7 _____

## Habit Linking

When you attach 1 new positive habit to another positive habit you're already used to doing regularly, you can increase the chances of implementing your new positive habit. Let's refer to that as "habit linking." For example, if you already brush your teeth daily in the evening, you might always complete a journal entry before you brush your teeth. In this case, you have, in essence, linked those 2 habits. What are 3 habits you would like to develop that you can add to already existing habits?

*Example:*

*Already existing positive habit:*          *New positive habit to add before or after:*
*Going to get my lunch from the fridge*   ⟶   *Taking a 10-minute walk (before/ after)*

Already existing positive habit:          New positive habit to add before or after:
_____ ⟶ _____ (before/ after)

Already existing positive habit:          New positive habit to add before or after:
_____ ⟶ _____ (before/ after)

Already existing positive habit:          New positive habit to add before or after:
_____ ⟶ _____ (before/ after)


## From Ripples to Waves: Sustaining Forward Movement

**Focus on continuous improvement.** As you're striving to be "becoming the ripple" to increase your influence in your personal and professional life, your ability to steadily increase your positive habits can make a significant difference on your path forward. Remember that we are all continuously improving and will all make mistakes along the way as we're growing and developing. When that happens, give yourself grace and keep moving forward. You may decide to revisit the exercises in this chapter every few months or even annually as you identify new habits to work on that can bring you closer to being the person you decide to be. Be sure to keep your greatest motivations in mind as you move forward.

When unsure of what to do next, just take the next small step. Even the most significant endeavors are completed through steady, step-by-step action.

# Reflections

_____

_____

_____

_____

_____

_____

_____

_____

_____

_____

_____

_____

_____

_____

_____

_____

_____

_____

_____

_____

_____

# PART TWO
# YOUR ACTION

# CHAPTER 4

# Explore What Truly Matters

*"If we take care of the moments, the years will take care of themselves."*

**—MARIA EDGEWORTH**

Do you find that your current schedule reflects your priorities? Part of our ability to be impactful professionally and personally has to do with keeping our priorities at the forefront of our time. This chapter will allow you time to reflect on and plan your optimal approach to your time as someone who is creating ripples of impact.

## Having a Values-Aligned Schedule

What are your **top 5 personal values** that are important to you and that you desire to see in your daily, weekly, monthly, or quarterly schedule?

*Example:*
*1. Integrity*
*2. Connecting to others*
*3. Legacy-building*
*4. Service*
*5. Self-care*

1. _____

2. _____

3. _____

4. _____

5. _____

What are your **top 5 professional values** that are important to you and that you desire to see in your daily, weekly, monthly, or quarterly schedule?

*Example:*
*1. Integrity*
*2. Connecting to others*
*3. Legacy-building (Succession planning)*
*4. Service*
*5. Showing care for self and others*

1. _____

2. _____

3. _____

4. _____

5. _____

## Roles and Goals Reflection

We have so many roles we play within and outside of work that influence how we approach our days, weeks, months, and even years. Use the activity below to explore ways that you desire to be intentional with your time in each of your roles.

First, you'll list 1 of your roles. For example: manager, caregiver, peer, friend, direct report, board member, sibling, project lead, etc. You can even choose to include various aspects of your position at work. For example: operations leader, strategist, compliance manager, inspirational leader, etc.

Then, you'll list 1 way you'd like to be more intentional with your time in this role.

*Example:*

***Role:*** <u>*Manager*</u>

*One way I'd like to be more intentional in this role on a daily, weekly, or monthly basis is:*
<u>*Take more time to understand the goals and motivations of my direct reports in our 1:1 check-ins.*</u>

*The date I'll start to implement this is:* <u>*October 25th*</u>

**Role #1:** _____

One way I'd like to be more intentional in this role on a daily, weekly, or monthly basis is:

_____

_____

_____

The date I'll start to implement this is: _____

**Role #2:** _____

One way I'd like to be more intentional in this role on a daily, weekly, or monthly basis is:

_____

_____

_____

The date I'll start to implement this is: _____

**Role #3:** _____

One way I'd like to be more intentional in this role on a daily, weekly, or monthly basis is:

_____

_____

_____

The date I'll start to implement this is: _____

## A Daily Planning Exercise

In order to be intentional around what you're accomplishing daily and weekly, set aside a specific timeframe each day where you're identifying where you are and where you'd like to be when it comes to your priorities each day. This can be a time when you examine how your values are aligning with your activities, where you decide to move action steps for the day or week ahead to a place on your calendar that's most effective for you, wrap up meeting notes, plan for the next day or week, or something else that allows you to feel most productive and purposeful.

What time of day might your daily planning take place? Some of the most popular timeframes to do this among my leadership development clients have been soon after they wake up, as soon as they get to their offices, before they leave work for the day, or before they go to sleep in the evenings.

The specific timeframe I will use for my daily planning time will be:

_____

---

**Write a check mark next to your top 3 - 5 daily planning activities you'd like to implement during your daily planning timeframe from the list below, or feel free to write in your own ideas.**

\_\_ Identify your top 3 recent wins

\_\_ Identify your top 3 things to do differently from recent observations

\_\_ Identify the #1 thing for you to do differently from recent observations

\_\_ Identify and reach out to 1 mentor to check in

\_\_ Identify and reach out to 1 colleague to check in

\_\_ Reach out to key stakeholders

\_\_ Check in on the status of key project(s) or initiative(s)

\_\_ Identify 1 - 3 priorities for the day ahead

\_\_ Divide your priorities into smaller action steps and time blocks

\_\_ Identify top tasks to delegate

\_\_ Clear your workspace

\_\_ Review your calendar and prepare for upcoming appointments, meetings, or events

\_\_ Review your calendar and shift when you will implement priorities

\_\_ Review your calendar and remove unnecessary action items

\_\_ Review your calendar and integrate 1 - 3 more things that align with your values

\_\_ List the top things that you're grateful for from recent observations

\_\_ Organize emails

\_\_ Respond to key emails

---

___ Schedule responding to specific emails
___ Read something energizing or inspiring
___ Read something to learn something new
___ Breathe, meditate, or pray

___ _____
___ _____
___ _____
___ _____
___ _____
___ _____

The date I'll start to implement this daily planning time in my schedule is:

_____

## Creating Your Ideal Weekly Plan

Reflect on what your ideal week would look like in order for you to feel you're living a life that is aligned with your greatest motivations. This is the schedule that could allow you to truly create ripples of impact for the things that matter most to you. What would your calendar look like if it integrated more of what you feel are your values and priorities? Below, sketch out what your ideal weekly plan would look like.

*Example of one day:*

|  | *Monday* |
|---|---|
| *5:30 a.m.* | *Wake up/ Pray/ Meditate* |
| *6:00 a.m.* | *Journaling/ Daily affirmations* |
| *6:30 a.m.* | *Exercise at the gym* |
| *7:00 a.m.* | *↓* |
| *7:30 a.m.* | *Breakfast* |
| *8:00 a.m.* | *Get ready to go to work* |
| *8:30 a.m.* | *Drive to work/ Call a family member* |
| *9:00 a.m.* | *Daily planning time and checking priority emails* |
| *10:00 a.m.* | *Completing top-priority work* |

| | |
|---|---|
| 10:30 a.m. | ↓ |
| 11:00 a.m. | ↓ |
| 11:30 a.m. | *Answering emails* |
| 12:00 p.m. | *Quick walk/ Lunch* |
| 12:30 p.m. | *Completing medium-priority work* |
| 1:00 p.m. | ↓ |
| 1:30 p.m. | *Completing lower-priority work* |
| 2:00 p.m. | ↓ |
| 2:30 p.m. | *Answering emails* |
| 3:00 p.m. | *Blocked time for uninterrupted work* |
| 3:30 p.m. | ↓ |
| 4:00 p.m. | |
| 4:30 p.m. | *Daily wrap-up time* |
| 5:00 p.m. | *Drive home/ Call a friend* |
| 5:30 p.m. | *Drinking water/ Eat prepared dinner* |
| 6:00 p.m. | *Watch TV/ Read/ Decompress* |
| 6:30 p.m. | ↓ |
| 7:00 p.m. | *Do personal errands* |
| 7:30 p.m. | ↓ |
| 8:00 p.m. | *Get ready to go to bed* |
| 8:30 p.m. | ↓ |
| 9:00 p.m. | *Read* |
| 9:30 p.m. | *Go to sleep* |
| 10:00 p.m. | ↓ |
| 10:30 p.m. | ↓ |

| | Sunday | Monday | Tuesday | Wednesday | Thursday | Friday | Saturday |
|---|---|---|---|---|---|---|---|
| **5:30 a.m.** | | | | | | | |
| **6:00 a.m.** | | | | | | | |
| **6:30 a.m.** | | | | | | | |

| | | | | | | |
|---|---|---|---|---|---|---|
| **7:00 a.m.** | | | | | | |
| **7:30 a.m.** | | | | | | |
| **8:00 a.m.** | | | | | | |
| **8:30 a.m.** | | | | | | |
| **9:00 a.m.** | | | | | | |
| **10:00 a.m.** | | | | | | |
| **10:30 a.m.** | | | | | | |
| **11:00 a.m.** | | | | | | |
| **11:30 a.m.** | | | | | | |
| **12:00 p.m.** | | | | | | |
| **12:30 p.m.** | | | | | | |
| **1:00 p.m.** | | | | | | |
| **1:30 p.m.** | | | | | | |

| | | | | | | |
|---|---|---|---|---|---|---|
| **2:00 p.m.** | | | | | | |
| **2:30 p.m.** | | | | | | |
| **3:00 p.m.** | | | | | | |
| **3:30 p.m.** | | | | | | |
| **4:00 p.m.** | | | | | | |
| **4:30 p.m.** | | | | | | |
| **5:00 p.m.** | | | | | | |
| **5:30 p.m.** | | | | | | |
| **6:00 p.m.** | | | | | | |
| **6:30 p.m.** | | | | | | |
| **7:00 p.m.** | | | | | | |
| **7:30 p.m.** | | | | | | |
| **8:00 p.m.** | | | | | | |

| | | | | | | |
|---|---|---|---|---|---|---|
| **8:30 p.m.** | | | | | | |
| **9:00 p.m.** | | | | | | |
| **9:30 p.m.** | | | | | | |
| **10:00 p.m.** | | | | | | |
| **10:30 p.m.** | | | | | | |

## From Ripples to Waves: Sustaining Forward Movement

**Approaching prioritization as a work in progress.** Your ability to increase your influence and impact is closely tied to how you manage your time on a regular basis. Weekly, schedule about 1 hour for you to adjust your calendar using your usual calendar tool(s). During these weekly calendar adjustment times, consider whether you might need to bring in a new tool to support your prioritization and planning, transition from using an organizational tool you're currently using, or enhance your approach to your current prioritization and planning tools. Over time, as you adjust regularly, you'll hone in on what organizational tools work best for you to make the most significant impact personally and professionally. My hopes are that you'll begin to see the ripples of impact that come from focusing on what's important through a practical approach to planning that shifts your days, weeks, months, *and years*.

Your time should reflect not
only your values but also
your desired impact.

# Reflections

# CHAPTER 5
# Practice Targeted Time

*"Either you run the day or
the day runs you."*

**—JIM ROHN**

Although we all have 24 hours in a day, it often seems like we don't have enough time to accomplish those things that we feel are most critical for our success, both personally and professionally. Part of being able to accomplish that is finding the timeframes within your day when you are most productive, somewhat productive, and moderately productive. We'll refer to these timeframes respectively as your primary focus time, secondary focus time, and tertiary focus time. Sometimes, you might have multiple time frames in one day that fit these categories.

## Identifying Your Most Effective Productivity Timeframes

Please list below what your one or two primary focus time(s), secondary focus time(s), and tertiary focus time(s) might be for you to best achieve your daily goals. List at least one timeframe for each category below.

*Example:*

*Primary Focus Time(s):*
*First Timeframe:*
*8:00 a.m. - 10:00 a.m.*

*Secondary Focus Time(s):*
*First Timeframe:*
*10:00 a.m. - 12:30 p.m.*
*Optional Second Timeframe:*
*1:00 p.m. - 3:00 p.m.*

*Tertiary Focus Time(s):*
*First Timeframe:*
*3:00 p.m. - 5:00 p.m.*

## Primary Focus Time(s) (your most productive daily timeframe):

First Timeframe:

[Start time] _____ to [End time] _____

Optional Second Timeframe:

[Start time] _____ to [End time] _____

Secondary Focus Time(s) (your somewhat productive daily timeframe):

First Timeframe:

[Start time] _____ to [End time] _____

Optional Second Timeframe:

[Start time] _____ to [End time] _____

Tertiary Focus Time(s) (your moderately productive daily timeframe):

First Timeframe:

[Start time] _____ to [End time] _____

Optional Second Timeframe:

[Start time] _____ to [End time] _____

If checking emails can be either a distraction for you or if checking emails is very important to your work (or a mixture of both), what are 1 - 3 timeframes that you desire to use for checking email?

*Example:*

*Email Management Timeframe 1:*
*9:00 a.m. - 10:00 a.m.*

*Email Management Timeframe 2:*
*12:30 p.m. - 1:00 p.m.*

*Email Management Timeframe 3:*
*4:30 p.m. - 5:00 p.m.*

*The date I'll start to implement this is: Wednesday, October 1st*

Email Management Timeframe 1:

[Start time] _____ to [End time] _____

Email Management Timeframe 2:

[Start time] _____ to [End time] _____

Email Management Timeframe 3:

[Start time] _____ to [End time] _____

The date I'll start to implement this is: _____

## Implementing the Right Tasks at the Right Times

Imagine that your daily prioritization is like a target. The bullseye on the target–that highest scoring zone–should represent the timeframe you work most effectively during your day. That's your "primary focus" timeframe. The times that are not the very best timeframes, but can still be effective for implementing your strategic goals, would be your "secondary focus" timeframe. The outside layer of the target could exemplify when your mind feels least productive, but where you still need to be somewhat productive. This area is what we will call "tertiary focus" time. This timeframe is for activities that do not require a complex level of strategic thought or are not as important, but still need to be accomplished. This framework for task prioritization is called Targeted Time.

Use the Targeted Time visual below to:

1. Write down your primary, secondary, and tertiary focus times from the previous exercise.
2. Write down in each relevant area below what 1-5 activities you feel are important to accomplish daily during your primary, secondary, and tertiary focus time for you to feel productive.

Example:

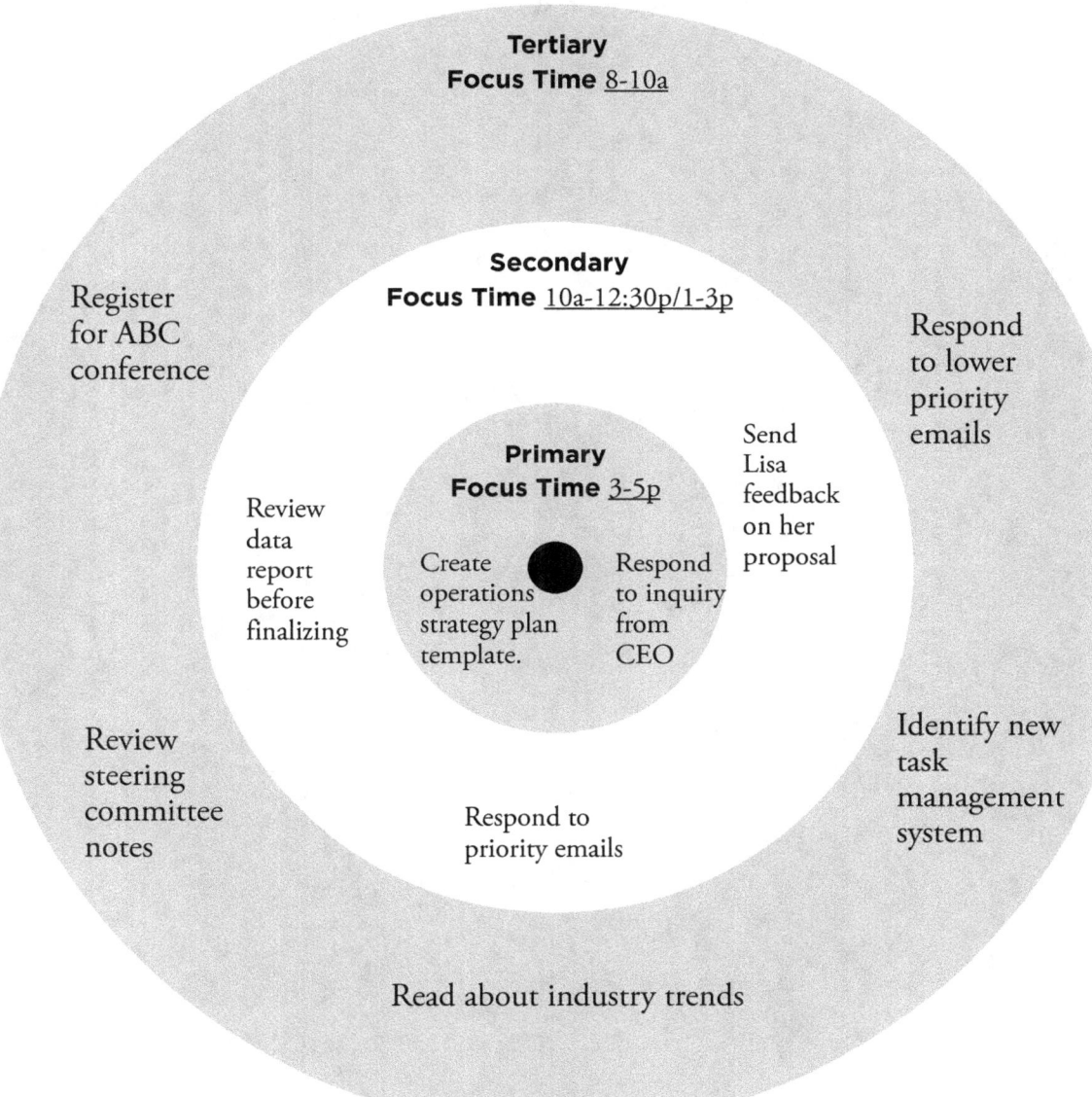

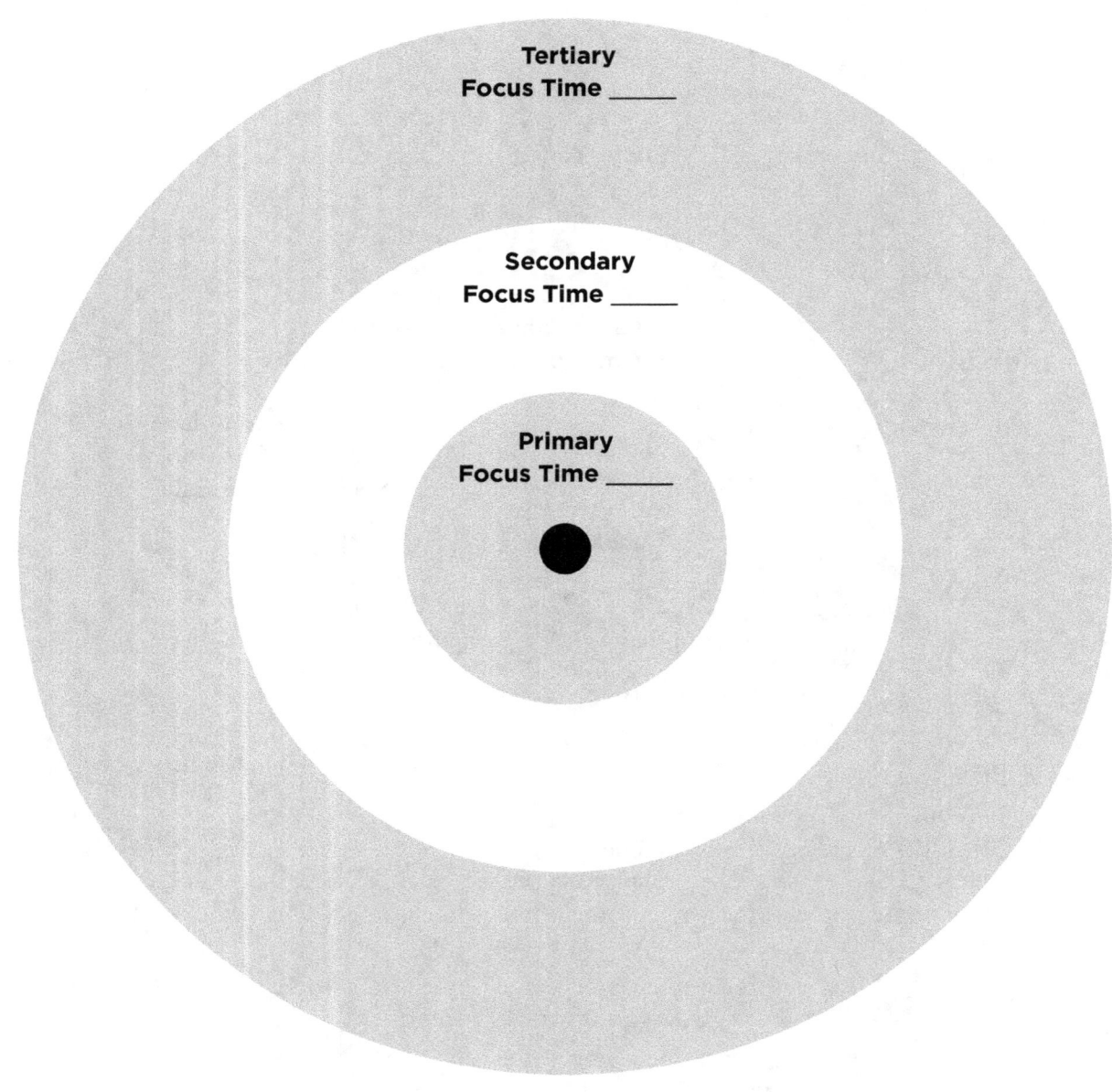

Tertiary
Focus Time _____

Secondary
Focus Time _____

Primary
Focus Time _____

## Developing Your Plan to Use Targeted Time

Regularly organizing your priorities can increase your chances of creating a significant impact in the areas that matter most to you or your organization. Some of our leadership development clients have found it helpful to use frameworks like Targeted Time daily or weekly to plan out priorities. Understanding how you'll use this framework and how frequently you'll use it are key to being able to utilize it well.

How frequently might you use this Targeted Time tool? Daily? Weekly? Monthly? One time?

_____

When would you start to use the Targeted Time tool?

_____

## From Ripples to Waves: Sustaining Forward Movement

**Add your Targeted Time priorities to your scheduling tool and adjust as needed.** Whether you use a digital or physical scheduling or reminder tool, find a way to physically have your Targeted Time priorities in front of you. And adjust your approach to Targeted Time as needed. You may find your initial scheduled primary focus time is not enough to complete your priorities, and needs to be placed into two blocks. You may find you never get to your tertiary focus time. Continue to shift and experiment with new ways of implementing your Targeted Time routine until you find what works best for you, your team, and your work culture.

Daily, identifying your primary, secondary, and tertiary objectives and tasks allows you to keep your eye on the prize.

# Reflections

# CHAPTER 6

# Use the Rule of 3s

*"Do what you can, with what you have, where you are."*

**—THEODORE ROOSEVELT**

Sometimes we have so many goals that we accomplish none of them or very little of them. This focus on too many things all at one time can also prevent us from accomplishing any of our goals. This chapter will help you focus on your top 3 most essential professional priorities, enabling you to create a greater impact and influence in your work.

## Clarifying Your Top 3 Goals

The following exercise will help you identify 3 professional goals that are most strategic and impactful for you to implement.

1. **Reflect on your buckets.** Think of all of the different components of your professional work (For example: strategy, operations, stakeholder management, etc.).
   a. **Identify your 3 main buckets.** If you had to split your work into just 3 buckets, considering what your most important work is, what would those be? Write down those 3 buckets in the table below.
   b. **Draft your priorities.** Then write your 5 - 10 most important activities or priorities associated with each of those buckets in the table below.

c. **Identify your top priorities.** Lastly, circle your top 3 most important activities or priorities associated with each bucket. You should have 9 top activities or priorities circled.

*Example:*

---

*Professional Work Bucket 1:*

*Stakeholder Management*

---

*5 - 10 Most Important Activities or Priorities Associated With This Bucket:*

*1. Sending status updates to board members quarterly*

*2. Drafting and sending letters to investors*

*3. Reaching out to do project status checks with key vendors*

*4. Revising team member project plans based on stakeholder knowledge*

*5. Meeting with key stakeholders regularly*

*6. _____*

*7. _____*

*8. _____*

*9. _____*

*10. _____*

---

| Professional Work Bucket 1: | Professional Work Bucket 2: | Professional Work Bucket 3: |
|---|---|---|
| _____ | _____ | _____ |
| 5 - 10 Most Important Activities or Priorities Associated With This Bucket: | 5 - 10 Most Important Activities or Priorities Associated With This Bucket: | 5 - 10 Most Important Activities or Priorities Associated With This Bucket: |
| 1._____ | 1._____ | 1._____ |
| 2._____ | 2._____ | 2._____ |
| 3._____ | 3._____ | 3._____ |
| 4._____ | 4._____ | 4._____ |
| 5._____ | 5._____ | 5._____ |
| 6._____ | 6._____ | 6._____ |
| 7._____ | 7._____ | 7._____ |
| 8._____ | 8._____ | 8._____ |
| 9._____ | 9._____ | 9._____ |
| 10._____ | 10._____ | 10._____ |

2. **Exploring the impact.** What would the impact be if you could focus on striving to consistently perform your top 3 activities or priorities for each bucket with excellence? What ripple effect might be caused for you and others around you if you were able to achieve that regularly?

*Example:*
*If I were able to achieve that regularly, I would see the results on my team drastically improve, and I would be more likely to attain a promotion sooner.*

_____

_____

_____

## Aligning Your Top Activities with Company Leadership and Culture

Part of growing your influence and impact is aligning your top activities and priorities with what matters most to your manager and the organization you work for. Being able to enhance your brand when it comes to your manager and organization can open up doors to new opportunities, result in a promotion, or even allow you to advocate more for yourself, those around you, or your customers. What would you consider your top 3 priorities overall for your role that resonate with what's most important to your manager and your company?

*Example:*
*1. Meeting with key stakeholders regularly.*
*2. Managing up to ensure the department is getting what it needs.*
*3. Successfully developing and implementing our strategic plan annually.*

1. _____

2. _____

3. _____


## Daily Gamechangers: Small, Game-Changing Acts of Consistency

Often, there are small steps we can take within our day that set us up for big successes. For example, if I am a sales professional and want to increase my number of sales conversations during my next day at work, I might close all the other tabs on my computer the evening before, except for my sales activities tab, to start doing sales activities the next morning. Suppose I were a university dean looking to ensure I contact key stakeholders who support our departmental efforts. In that case, I might block off my calendar for no internal meetings between 11 a.m. and 12 p.m. daily, allowing me to focus solely on outreach to key stakeholders during that timeframe.

What are 3 recurring actions that could contribute greatly to you achieving your top 3 overall priorities in your work regularly? These are your daily gamechangers.

*Example:*
*1. Updating my project management system daily.*
*2. Implementing uninterrupted hours between 11 a.m. and 12 p.m. for priority work.*
*3. Scheduling time daily at the beginning of the day for meeting preparation.*

1. _____

2. _____

3. _____

## Three Key Conversations

To ensure we're on the right track with our priorities, we sometimes need to engage in conversations with individuals within or outside our workplaces to gain clarity, support, or feedback on our top priorities. These exchanges don't just benefit you. They help others around us within our organizations to create ripples of impact, as we create our own.

In some work cultures, seeking mentorship or advice from colleagues within your organization may not be considered appropriate, or you may lack trusted mentors, advisors, sponsors, or coaches to discuss your priorities with. If that is the case, I urge you to develop relationships with a few trusted individuals internally and externally to gain the clarity, support, or feedback you need in the future.

If you were to have at least 3 conversations with 3 different individuals to gain clarity, support, or feedback on your top priorities, who would those key individuals be, and what are the outcomes that you would desire for each conversation?

*Example:*
***Key Stakeholder #1:*** *John Doe, our COO*

*Desired Key Conversation Outcome:*
*I hope to understand what John Doe feels are our strengths and areas for growth for our company's operations, and how my work can contribute to addressing our company's areas for growth.*

**Key Stakeholder #1:** _____

Desired Key Conversation Outcome:

_____

_____

_____

**Key Stakeholder #2:** _____

Desired Key Conversation Outcome:

_____

_____

_____


**Key Stakeholder #3:** _____

Desired Key Conversation Outcome:

_____

_____

_____


## Three-Month Priority Check-in Plan

In the previous section of this workbook titled "Aligning your top activities with company leadership and culture", you identified your top three priorities. In order to keep track of your progress on those priorities, identify what your milestones might be over the next 3 months that will enable you to perform your top priorities with excellence.

*Example:*

| |
|---|
| **Priority 1:** *Meeting with key stakeholders regularly* |
| **30-Day Milestone:** *Identify key stakeholders who are essential to meet with regularly and a specific meeting cadence for each key stakeholder. Identify the right system to remind me that those meetings should be scheduled and that tracks when they are scheduled.* |
| **60-Day Milestone:** *Based on key stakeholder feedback, complete a key stakeholder meeting audit, what's going well with key stakeholder meetings, what could be better, and how can meeting content, structure, and other associated logistics be adjusted?* |
| **90-Day Milestone:** *Implement a new key stakeholder meeting approach and key stakeholder meeting tracking system to meet regularly with key stakeholders.* |

| Priority 1: |
| --- |
| **30-Day Milestone:** |
| **60-Day Milestone:** |
| **90-Day Milestone:** |

| Priority 2: |
| --- |
| **30-Day Milestone:** |
| **60-Day Milestone:** |
| **90-Day Milestone:** |

| Priority 3: |
| --- |
| **30-Day Milestone:** |
| **60-Day Milestone:** |
| **90-Day Milestone:** |

## From Ripples to Waves: Sustaining Forward Movement

**Quarterly priority planning time.** Quarterly, you can use the exercises associated with the rule of 3's to hone in on your top priorities even when you have a full plate of priorities at work. Even if you very informally reflect on what the most essential 3 goals are that are associated with your work, it will allow you to hone in on what truly is most important for you to enhance your influence and impact at work to create the ripple effect you might be striving to create. Doing this exercise regularly will allow you to consistently be focused on what's most essential and can drastically impact the way you approach your life and its priorities.

Even when your plate is full,
your priorities are still few.
Clarifying priorities provides you
with a pathway to your vision.

# Reflections

# PART 3
# YOUR VOICE

# CHAPTER 7

# Remember Your 3 Keys

*"Courage is the most important of all the virtues because, without courage, you can't practice any other virtue consistently."*

**—MAYA ANGELOU**

Though you might know your "why" and are focusing on your top priorities to pursue professional success, if you are perceived negatively by others, it can cause conflict, confusion, frustration, or even cause you to be treated as less valuable at work. This can create a ripple effect that is actually a negative one, and if you're utilizing this workbook, I'm sure that creating a negative ripple effect is not your intention. Instead, exploring who we are at our best and amplifying that exponentially increases our chances of creating a ripple effect that boosts our influence and impact, ultimately leading to our success and the success of those around us.

## Who Do Others Say You Are?

In order to identify who you are at your best, it can be helpful to reflect on how you have been when you have worked best with your colleagues, been most successful working in groups, or contributed to things going well with you and your managers.

There is a saying of unknown origin that, "You cannot see the picture if you're in the frame." This is why gaining other perspectives, beyond our own, on our unique strengths is so important. In this exercise, you will ask about 3 - 10 of your friends, family, or work colleagues, "How am I when I am at my best?" This will allow you to gain some insights about what you embody when others perceive you to be at your best.

Write below what your friends, family, or colleagues said when you asked them, "How am I when I am at my best?"

*Example:*
*Lisa, my friend - You are a natural problem solver.*
*John, my colleague at a previous job - You always seem to find levity and bring hope to any situation, even in the most challenging circumstances.*
*Amy, my manager - I love the way you lead your team. You treat them like family, yet you hold them to high expectations.*
*Jill, my cousin - Ever since we were young, you've always known how to bring the energy and fun to wherever you are, but you also know how to be serious when it's time to be serious.*

_____

_____

_____

_____

_____

_____

_____

_____

_____

_____

_____

What would you say are the top 3 themes that stood out from the exercise above when it came to the responses you noted in the previous answer?

*Example:*
*Theme 1: Energy - Multiple people mentioned that I bring energy or fun into situations.*
*Theme 2: Connectedness - Several people shared that I'm able to connect with different kinds of people, no matter their age or background, personally or professionally.*
*Theme 3: Follow-through - People seemed to say in different ways that I get things done, no matter the challenges that come my way.*

_____

_____

_____

_____

_____

_____

_____

_____

_____

_____

_____

_____

## Who Do You Want to Be? An Ideal Perception Brainstorm

You heard from those who are in your circle, and now you'll explore for yourself what you desire to exude when you're at your best. In the following exercise, you'll take time to brainstorm what you would desire others to perceive you as ideally. Think of your governing principles—phrases that embody how you feel it's best to operate—like "clarity is kind," "to whom much is given, much is required," or "remember your intentions," for example, as you reflect on what you aspire to exude daily.

1. **Create a list.** Create a list of 15 words or phrases that embody who you are personally and professionally when you are at your best. Be sure that these words truly resonate with you and your values.

a. **Star your top 7.** Write a star next to the top 7 words or phrases that embody who you are personally and professionally when you are at your best.

b. **Underline your top 3.** Underline the top 3 words or phrases that embody who you are personally and professionally when you are at your best. These are your 3 keys.

*Example:*
1. *Follow-through*
2. *Achiever**
3. *Hopeful*
4. *Energetic*
5. *Problem-solver**
6. *Connected**
7. *Analytical*
8. *Mentor**
9. *Forward-thinking**
10. *Creative*
11. *Compassionate*
12. *Empathetic**
13. *Present*
14. *Inspirational leader**
15. *Thoughtful*

1. _____

2. _____

3. _____

4. _____

5. _____

6. _____

7. _____

8. _____

9. _____

10. _____

11. _____

12. _____

13. _____

14. _____

15. _____

2.  The 3 words or phrases that you chose are your "3 Keys". Why are the 3 words or phrases that you chose meaningful to you?

*Example:*

*Problem-solver - It's essential in my role as an operations leader that I know how to identify problems and solve them swiftly. How I do this work impacts our organization as a whole, and I want to ensure I do this work well.*

*Mentor - I've always been inclined to support others to achieve their goals and dreams. Being a mentor to colleagues and being a great learner and mentee are extremely important and meaningful to me. I've come to realize that helping direct reports be their best has a broader impact on the team and our ability to meet our objectives.*

*Inspirational leader - To me, being a leader means very little if I'm not leading in a way that aligns with my character and values. I'm aware that the way I show up creates some sort of impact, and even as I hold others to high expectations, I want that impact to be a meaningful one.*

_____

_____

_____

_____

_____

_____

_____

3.  For each of your 3 Keys, write about 1 example where you embodied that word or phrase in a professional setting in the past:

*Example:*

**1. First keyword or phrase:** *Problem-solver*

*One example of when you embodied that word or phrase in the past:*

*After reviewing our Q3 operations report with my direct reports, I identified three team action steps that could reduce our company's expenses by $3 million in the current fiscal year, leveraging my ability to anticipate potential issues and devise feasible solutions.*

**1. First keyword or phrase:** _____

One example of when you embodied that word or phrase in the past:

_____

_____

_____

**2. Second keyword or phrase:** _____

One example of when you embodied that word or phrase in the past:

_____

_____

_____

3. Third keyword or phrase: _____

One example of when you embodied that word or phrase in the past:

_____

_____

_____

## Assessing your Current Alignment with your 3 Keys

Rate on a scale of 1 - 5 how aligned you currently are professionally for each of your 3 Keys, with 5 being you're completely aligned with each of your 3 Keys and 1 being you're not at all aligned. Explain why you rated yourself the way you did.

| Your 3 Keys | On a scale of 1 - 5, how aligned are you currently with this Key professionally, with 5 being you're completely aligned and 1 being you're not at all aligned? | Why did you give yourself this rating? |
| --- | --- | --- |
| **Key 1:**<br><br>*Example: Problem-solver* | *Example: 4* | *Example: Though I currently strive to be responsive to others' requests for me to analyze or create plans, I feel I can increase how proactive I am about exploring aspects of our company that could be made more efficient.* |
| **Key 2:** | | |
| **Key 3:** | | |

Based on your ratings and explanations above, where did you see that you're currently most aligned with your 3 Keys, and where do you feel you might need to be more intentional? What can you do to be more intentional?

_____

_____

_____

_____

_____

List 1 way you can use each of your 3 Keys to increase your influence or impact at work.

*Example:*

*1. First keyword or phrase: <u>Problem-solver</u>*

*If you are more aligned with this word or phrase, how would that increase your influence or impact at work?*

*<u>If I'm more proactive about problem-solving, this would position me more as a key decision-maker and leader who creates even more impact at work.</u>*

**1. First key word or phrase:** _____

If you are more aligned with this word or phrase, how would that increase your influence or impact at work?

_____

_____

_____

**2. Second key word or phrase:** _____

If you are more aligned with this word or phrase, how would that increase your influence or impact at work?

_____

_____

_____

**3. Third key word or phrase:** _____

If you are more aligned with this word or phrase, how would that increase your influence or impact at work?

_____

_____

_____

## Your 3 Keys Weekly Tracker

Use the table below to identify 3 - 5 small or more involved actions that you can take daily to try to be more intentional around each of your 3 Keys.

| Your 3 Keys | What are 3 - 5 small or involved actions you can do daily to try to be intentional around each of your 3 Keys? | How will you remember to try to be intentional around this Key daily? |
|---|---|---|
| **Key 1:**<br><br>*Example: Problem-solver* | *Example:*<br>*1. Share during meetings that I'm willing to contribute to complex projects as they come up.*<br>*2. Tell myself, "I am completely equipped to handle this" when a challenge comes my way, remembering I have resources externally and internally to solve problems.*<br>*3. Network to have more problem-solvers as mentors and closer colleagues at work and outside of work to hone my skillset.* | *Example:*<br>*1. Schedule a calendar reminder to remind me to contribute to problem-solving at meetings that will be set before meetings.*<br>*2. Set a daily reminder each morning with affirmations, including this one.*<br>*3. Schedule to connect with or cultivate a relationship with someone at work and to attend monthly networking events.* |
| **Key 2:** | | |
| **Key 3:** | | |

Then, use a tracker like the one below to check off each day that you tried to be intentional about implementing each of your 3 Keys, either by implementing 1 of the actions above or some other actions. Feel free to use the tracker below or create your own!

**Your 3 Keys Weekly Tracker**

| Your 3 Keys | Sunday | Monday | Tuesday | Wednesday | Thursday | Friday | Saturday |
|---|---|---|---|---|---|---|---|
| **Key 1:** | | | | | | | |
| **Key 2:** | | | | | | | |
| **Key 3:** | | | | | | | |

## Your 3 Keys Affirmations

What is 1 affirmation or mantra that you can create to say daily about each of your 3 Keys individually or combined that might help you to strive to be intentional around your 3 Keys?

*Example: Key 1: Problem-solver - I am equipped to solve every challenge.*

_____

_____

_____

_____

Where will you place your 3 Keys or your 3 Keys affirmations or mantra in order to have a visual reminder of your 3 Keys? Some examples of where you can place them are:

- ○ On a sticky note in a prominent location
- ○ As a pop-up daily or weekly reminder on your phone
- ○ In a calendar invite that comes up daily or weekly on your phone or computer
- ○ As a home screen on your phone or computer

_____

_____

## From Ripples to Waves: Sustaining Forward Movement

**Your 3 Keys integration check:** We all have different experiences, backgrounds, and lenses that cause each of us to have a unique way of "becoming the ripple" personally or professionally. When each of us consistently focuses on *our own* 3 Keys, it can help transform how we show up professionally as we more frequently embody our best selves and benefit from the rewards of what that produces personally and professionally in our lives.

To help you determine if you're consistently integrating your 3 Keys, periodically, you can schedule in your calendar "Your 3 Keys integration check." When you see that pop up in your calendar, you can choose a recent email, meeting, or presentation to reflect on.

For that email, meeting, or presentation that you chose, assess if your communication reflected any of your 3 Keys and identify how you can be more aligned with your 3 Keys in that communication in the future.

How we show up in the world not only impacts our professional possibilities but can also impact our peace, productivity, and purpose.

# Reflections

_____

_____

_____

_____

_____

_____

_____

_____

_____

_____

_____

_____

_____

_____

_____

_____

_____

_____

_____

_____

# CHAPTER 8

# Be Who You Aspire to Be

*"Show up, show up, show up, and after a while, the muse shows up, too."*

**—ISABEL ALLENDE**

*"Live out of your imagination, not your history."*

**—STEPHEN COVEY**

Personally and professionally, we all have circumstances that can make it challenging to regularly aspire to be our best selves. Sometimes our personal or professional backgrounds hinder us from always exuding the confidence, peace, or productivity we'd like. Or maybe you're a caretaker or juggling several responsibilities. We have a choice, even in the most challenging circumstances, to either try to be more of who we aspire to be or decide that this isn't possible or within our capacity. I hope that as you delve into this chapter, you'll gain some tangible tools to help you see how you can practically be more of who it is that you aspire to be as you are "becoming the ripple" professionally and personally.

## Going Back to Your "Why"

Below, write about your "why." What inspires you to be your best self in your work, relationships, and leadership, even when challenges come your way?

*Example:*

*My older cousin and all that she instilled in me as I grew up inspires me to be the same kind of leader that I saw her be at work and at home. She embodies many of the characteristics I aspire to as a leader, including the ability to be consistent for all of these years. I've seen the significant impact of her character and am regularly inspired to work and lead in the same way.*

_____

_____

_____

## 3 Keys Journal Prompt

Answer the following prompts, and afterwards, use a digital document or physical journal to answer the following prompts weekly. These prompts can contribute to you being most aligned with who you are when you're at your best, for you to create the ripple of impact that you desire both personally and professionally:

Where did I feel that I was most aligned with my 3 Keys this week?

*Example: I was most aligned with my 3 Keys this week during my 1:1 meeting with my direct report, my strategic planning work independently, and my discussion with my colleague about our project.*

_____

_____

_____

When did I feel least aligned with my 3 Keys this week?

*Example: I was least aligned with my 3 Keys this week when having a difficult conversation with my manager about something I disagreed with.*

_____

_____

_____

What contributed to when I felt most or least aligned, and what will I shift next week?

*Example: I realize that I need to be more aligned with my values during difficult conversations. Next week, I'll be more proactive about preparing how I want to show up in meetings, especially those that have had difficult topics come up in the past. I need to keep in mind the leader I'm aspiring to be, even when it's hard, and why that's important to me.*

_____

_____

_____

## In-the-Moment 3 Keys Alignment Reset

There will be times when you realize that you are not operating in alignment with your 3 Keys. Though in those moments, there may be affirmations, words, questions, or other practices that you can use to shift. Some examples are:

- "Take 3 deep breaths."
- "How would I *be* right now if operating with my 3 Keys?"
- "Pause and choose *well*."

What are 3 different affirmations, words, questions, or other practices that you can use to help you shift when you're feeling misaligned?

1. _____

2. _____

3. _____

## Reframing Setbacks: A Win or a Lesson?

Reflect on a previous time when you were not feeling like you were exuding the best version of yourself. Think about what you learned from that moment. If you think about situations as a win or a lesson, how can you reframe that moment as part of your growth rather than a failure or loss?

*Example: When I realized I was not exuding the best version of myself in a difficult conversation with my manager, I realized that there are triggers that cause me to act a certain way that I don't want to act that I need to work through. It taught me that I still have some work to do when it comes to my own personal and professional devel-*

*opment. I'd like to read books and seek out professional support to understand the root of those triggers and what I can do to adjust my natural responses to them.*

_____

_____

_____

_____

_____

_____

## A 30-Day Challenge to Expand Your Ripple

For the next 30 days, what is 1 habit that, if done consistently, can make you feel that you're operating more consistently with your 3 Keys in mind?

*Taking a deep breath and sharing in my mind an affirmation or reminder helps me navigate conversations when I start to feel anxious, overwhelmed, frustrated, or something else that's not in alignment.*

_____

_____

## From Ripples to Waves: Sustaining Forward Movement

**Utilize an accountability partner and/or scheduled check-ins:** To sustain forward movement when it comes to your 3 Keys, you can find someone who you trust to be your accountability partner. This can be a team member, your manager, a colleague from another department, or even a family member or friend with whom you might discuss specific professional challenges or opportunities. You can share your 3 keys with this person and ask them if they are willing to check in with you about how you are doing when it comes to your 3 Keys on a weekly or monthly basis, or at some other frequency you decide upon. If you work in close proximity to your accountability partner, you can ask your accountability partner to observe your actions and approaches regularly. You would also ask them to share feedback about your alignment with your 3 Keys, which can help you be more aligned with your values. Your accountability partner can be a mentor, advisor, friend, therapist, or someone else.

Even if you choose not to have an accountability partner, establishing a regularly occurring journaling routine or a scheduled time periodically to check in with yourself daily or weekly can be priceless. During this time, you can identify where you can better align with your values and determine what you can do to get closer to where you want to be when it comes to "becoming the ripple" in your life and work.

The uneasy feeling you might get when you don't feel in alignment may just be a sign that it's time to get back on track.

# Reflections

# CHAPTER 9

# Analyze Your Tone

*"What you do speaks so loudly that*
*I cannot hear what you say."*

**—RALPH WALDO EMERSON**

Every individual who has the ability to influence others uses their unique style and approach to create that influence. Your approach to influencing might use humor, deep listening, charisma, or something else, for example. What is critically important when it comes to our tone is how much we're able to utilize our approach in conversations to create influence for any key stakeholder we're interacting with.

## Stakeholder Tone Mapping

In the exercise below, you'll identify 5 key stakeholders for you professionally and rate your level of effective communication with each. You'll come up with a Tone Effectiveness Rating for each key stakeholder below.

*Example:*

**Key Stakeholder #1 Name:** <u>John Doe (My manager)</u>

*Please rate the different aspects of your communication with this key stakeholder below, using a scale from 1 (not at all effective) to 10 (very effective) in each area.*

- *My communication always results in positive outcomes with this individual 7*
- *My communication with this individual exudes confidence 8*
- *My communication with this individual creates more collaboration than conflict 9*
- *My communication enables me to be respected by this individual 8*
- *My communication enables me to be trusted by this individual 10*
- *My communication enables this individual to effectively provide me with feedback 9*
- *My communication enables this individual to effectively share new ideas with me 8*
- *My communication establishes healthy boundaries with this individual 6*

*Add the ratings above for this key stakeholder together and divide by 8 to find what your overall tone effectiveness rating is with this key stakeholder. Average rating: 8.125*

*What 3 action steps can you implement to take your tone effectiveness rating with this stakeholder up 1 notch?*

*1. Learning more about my manager's motivations to be able to experience more positive outcomes in our conversations/ 2. Remembering my 3 Keys to show up more confidently/ 3. Use healthier professional boundaries in our interactions (for example, trying not to exchange late-night emails when unnecessary).*

## Key Stakeholder #1 Name: _____

Please rate the different aspects of your communication with this key stakeholder below, using a scale from 1 (not at all effective) to 10 (very effective) in each area:

- My communication always results in positive outcomes with this individual ___
- My communication with this individual exudes confidence ___
- My communication with this individual creates more collaboration than conflict ___
- My communication enables me to be respected by this individual ___
- My communication enables me to be trusted by this individual ___
- My communication enables this individual to effectively provide me with feedback ___
- My communication enables this individual to effectively share new ideas with me ___
- My communication establishes healthy boundaries with this individual ___

Add the ratings above for this key stakeholder together and divide by 8 to find what your overall tone effectiveness rating is with this key stakeholder. Average rating: ___

What 3 action steps can you implement to take your tone effectiveness rating with this stakeholder up 1 notch?

_____

_____

_____

**Key Stakeholder #2 Name:** _____

Please rate the different aspects of your communication with this key stakeholder below, using a scale from 1 (not at all effective) to 10 (very effective) in each area.

- My communication always results in positive outcomes with this individual ___
- My communication with this individual exudes confidence ___
- My communication with this individual creates more collaboration than conflict ___
- My communication enables me to be respected by this individual ___
- My communication enables me to be trusted by this individual ___
- My communication enables this individual to effectively provide me with feedback ___
- My communication enables this individual to effectively share new ideas with me ___
- My communication establishes healthy boundaries with this individual ___

Add the ratings above for this key stakeholder together and divide by 8 to find what your overall tone effectiveness rating is with this key stakeholder. Average rating: ___

What 3 action steps can you implement to take your tone effectiveness rating with this stakeholder up 1 notch? _____

_____

_____

**Key Stakeholder #3 Name:** _____

Please rate the different aspects of your communication with this key stakeholder below, using a scale from 1 (not at all effective) to 10 (very effective) in each area.

- My communication always results in positive outcomes with this individual ___
- My communication with this individual exudes confidence ___
- My communication with this individual creates more collaboration than conflict ___
- My communication enables me to be respected by this individual ___
- My communication enables me to be trusted by this individual ___
- My communication enables this individual to effectively provide me with feedback ___
- My communication enables this individual to effectively share new ideas with me ___
- My communication establishes healthy boundaries with this individual ___

Add the ratings above for this key stakeholder together and divide by 8 to find what your overall tone effectiveness rating is with this key stakeholder. Average rating: ___

What 3 action steps can you implement to take your tone effectiveness rating with this stakeholder up 1 notch? _____

_____

_____

**Key Stakeholder #4 Name:**_____

Please rate the different aspects of your communication with this key stakeholder below, using a scale from 1 (not at all effective) to 10 (very effective) in each area.

- My communication always results in positive outcomes with this individual ___
- My communication with this individual exudes confidence ___
- My communication with this individual creates more collaboration than conflict ___
- My communication enables me to be respected by this individual ___
- My communication enables me to be trusted by this individual ___
- My communication enables this individual to effectively provide me with feedback ___
- My communication enables this individual to effectively share new ideas with me ___
- My communication establishes healthy boundaries with this individual ___

Add the ratings above for this key stakeholder together and divide by 8 to find what your overall tone effectiveness rating is with this key stakeholder. Average rating: ___

What 3 action steps can you implement to take your tone effectiveness rating with this stakeholder up 1 notch? _____

_____

_____

**Key Stakeholder #5 Name:**_____

Please rate the different aspects of your communication with this key stakeholder below, using a scale from 1 (not at all effective) to 10 (very effective) in each area.

- My communication always results in positive outcomes with this individual ___
- My communication with this individual exudes confidence ___
- My communication with this individual creates more collaboration than conflict ___
- My communication enables me to be respected by this individual ___
- My communication enables me to be trusted by this individual ___
- My communication enables this individual to effectively provide me with feedback ___

- My communication enables this individual to effectively share new ideas with me ___
- My communication establishes healthy boundaries with this individual ___

Add the ratings above for this key stakeholder together and divide by 8 to find what your overall tone effectiveness rating is with this key stakeholder. Average rating: ___

What 3 action steps can you implement to take your tone effectiveness rating with this stakeholder up 1 notch?

1. _____

2. _____

3. _____

## Conducting a Tone Audit

Reflect on 5 professional conversations you've had this past week. Assess the tone you used in those conversations and the outcome. How was your tone? Was it mostly assertive, calm, humorous, defensive, passive, engaged, disengaged, or something else? What impact did that have?

| Who was the conversation with? What was it about? | What was your predominant tone within the conversation? | What impact did your tone have in this conversation? |
|---|---|---|
| 1) *Example: Conversation with my colleague about our talent development committee work* | *Example: Assertive and calm* | *Example: My tone created a clear path forward, but didn't build very much rapport with my colleague as I'd like.* |
| 2) | | |
| 3) | | |
| 4) | | |
| 5) | | |

What would you have changed, if anything at all, when it comes to your tone in any of the conversations you mentioned above?

*Example: I would have made more time in formal conversations to build rapport, ensured I remained calmer in the most difficult conversations, and been more curious by asking more questions in certain conversations.*

_____

_____

_____

What are 3 potential actions you can take to enhance your tone with different individuals in the coming week?

*Example:*

*1. With Lisa, my colleague, I will spend a few minutes at the beginning of our next meeting to build rapport.*

1. _____

2. _____

3. _____

## Your "Ideal Tone" Affirmation

Write a short affirmation, mantra, or script below that you can repeat to yourself periodically or regularly that reflects what you would like to exude in key conversations.

*Example: I speak with calm, resolve, and clarity and strive to listen with curiosity more than I speak to be right.*

_____

_____

_____

## From Ripples to Waves: Sustaining Forward Movement

**Repeating your stakeholder tone mapping exercise:** To be "becoming the ripple" takes for us to regularly assess where we are and where we'd like to be when it comes to how we're showing up in the world. After completing the exercises above, you should ideally see a shift in how you're strategically taking ownership of how you're showing up with key stakeholders. At least 30 days after implementing your first stakeholder tone mapping exercise from this chapter, go through this process again to evaluate how you now feel about your tone with key stakeholders. Schedule a recurring calendar invite to regularly assess how you're showing up to those key stakeholders who are critically important in your roles, both professionally and personally.

Take ownership of how you're showing up in the world by regularly being intentional about who you are inside and out.

# Reflections

_____

_____

_____

_____

_____

_____

_____

_____

_____

_____

_____

_____

_____

_____

_____

_____

_____

_____

_____

# PART 4
# YOUR ENVIRONMENT

# CHAPTER 10

# Be a Culture Changer

*"You can get everything in life you want if you will just help enough other people get what they want."*

**—ZIG ZIGLAR**

In many organizations, there are a few people who stand out as essential to the organization. We'll call them "culture changers." People often want to be on the team of culture changers, even if a culture changer has high expectations for their teams, and managers know culture changers get things done. Sometimes, culture changers might be those who truly define that workplace as having an energetic, driven, or inclusive culture. Culture changers' absence is felt when they transition from teams, and when a culture changer is on your team, you can feel it, too.

## Examples of Culture Changers

Reflect on culture changers who you have encountered in your professional life—or research professionals who have shifted the culture of their organizations or industry. Share about 3 of those culture changers below.

*Example:*

*Culture changer #1 name, career role, and industry:*

*John Doe, CEO, Tech*

*What traits or behaviors supported this culture changer to create change? What impact did they have?*

*The traits or behaviors that supported John to create change were his inspirational leadership, ability to transform struggling teams into highly effective teams, consistent attention to data and results, and ability to communicate challenging news in a way that built trust and brought people together.*

*What are your top 3 lessons or takeaways from reflecting on or researching this culture changer?*

*1. I need to focus as much on my ability to cultivate respect and rapport from my direct reports as I do on making sure our team meets or exceeds metrics/ 2. Any team has the potential to thrive, especially if it has the right team members and can effectively guide them. How you communicate is just as important as what you communicate.*

**Culture changer #1 name, career role, and industry:**

_____

What traits or behaviors supported this culture changer to create change? What impact did they have?

_____

_____

_____

What are your top 3 lessons or takeaways from reflecting on or researching this culture changer?

_____

_____

_____

_____

**Culture changer #2 name, career role, and industry:**

_____

What traits or behaviors supported this culture changer to create change? What impact did they have?

_____

_____

_____

What are your top 3 lessons or takeaways from reflecting on or researching this culture changer?

_____

_____

_____

_____

_____

**Culture changer #3 name, career role, and industry:**

_____

What traits or behaviors supported this culture changer to create change? What impact did they have?

_____

_____

_____

What are your top 3 lessons or takeaways from reflecting on or researching this culture changer?

_____

_____

_____

_____

## Why Become a Culture Changer?

Being a culture changer allows you to expand your influence and impact. Your ability to be a culture changer can result in more opportunities, more professional mentors or sponsors, or even greater career growth as you're placed on teams and in rooms, roles, and organizations that your contributions can impact. It also allows you to have a greater impact on the growth and success of initiatives that you're contributing to. The impact you can have on your organization, your community, and society is truly limitless as a culture changer.

Reflect on your "why" and your overall greatest motivations for "becoming the ripple" professionally and personally. What are your greatest motivations for being a culture changer at work? If you already consider yourself a culture changer at work, what are your reasons for expanding your impact as a culture changer?

*Example:*

*My greatest motivations for being a culture changer at work are to be an example for my children, to be able to impact the lives of all of those who I work with, and to continue the legacy of impact and leadership from my family members I looked up to as I was growing up.*

_____

_____

_____

_____

_____

_____

## Why Now is the Time to Become a Culture Changer

For those who are culture changers, often an event or inspiration happens at some point in their lives that sparks their desire to take their contributions to the next level. They then have a desire to implement action steps to become a culture changer, and then they go about implementing those action steps. Often, this cycle happens over and over in the life of a culture changer.

**The event.** What is an event or inspiration that has happened at some point in your personal or professional life that has led you to desire to be a culture changer?

*Example:*
*I met a mentor in one of my first jobs who shared with me that he thought some day I would lead an organization and that he would help to equip me to do just that. It completely changed my perspective on who I would be in the future.*

_____

_____

_____

**The desire to act.** How would you desire to create impact as a culture changer?

*Example:*
*I desire to create impact as a culture changer through making sure I model the behaviors I want to see in the people around me at work and home.*

_____

_____

_____

**The implementation.** How can you remember to regularly be taking action to be a culture changer?

*Example:*
*I can create a reminder in my Google Calendar each morning that has an affirmation that reminds me to regularly be taking action that is aligned with me being a culture changer.*

_____

_____

_____

## Your Village for Impact

Reflect on who should be in your circle of trusted advisors, that we'll call your village, for you to enhance your ability to be a culture changer. Think about the mentors, sponsors, and colleagues you would like to be a part of your career growth. Consider adding a coach, therapist, and other roles to your key stakeholder list of those you think might provide additional insights or accountability. For each prospective trusted advisor, define 1 step that you can take to deepen your relationship with this person. These can be individuals who are already in your village or those you want to be a part of your village.

*Example:*

**Prospective trusted advisor #1:** *Jane Doe*

*What's 1 small step that you can take to deepen your relationship (e.g., send an email, ask for a coffee chat, ask for mentorship, ask for a meeting, ask to chat, affirm a recent achievement, participate in their initiative, etc.)*

*I can ask for a coffee chat.*

*What would be your greatest intention with this trusted advisor?*

*My greatest intention would be to build rapport and eventually be able to ask for advice quarterly on things that are most pressing for me as a leader, while also somehow being able to be a valuable resource to her as well.*

**Prospective trusted advisor #1:** _____

What's 1 small step that you can take to deepen your relationship (e.g., send an email, ask for a coffee chat, ask for mentorship, ask for a meeting, ask to chat, affirm a recent achievement, participate in their initiative, etc.)

_____

What would be your greatest intention with this trusted advisor?

_____

_____

**Prospective trusted advisor #2:** _____

What's 1 small step you can take to deepen your relationship (e.g., send an email, ask for a coffee chat, ask for mentorship, ask for a meeting, ask to chat, affirm a recent achievement, participate in their initiative, etc.)

_____

What would be your greatest intention with this trusted advisor?

_____

_____

**Prospective trusted advisor #3:** _____

What's 1 small step you can take to deepen your relationship (e.g., send an email, ask for a coffee chat, ask for mentorship, ask for a meeting, ask to chat, affirm a recent achievement, participate in their initiative, etc.)

_____

What would be your greatest intention with this trusted advisor?

_____

_____

**Prospective trusted advisor #4:** _____

What's 1 small step you can take to deepen your relationship (e.g., send an email, ask for a coffee chat, ask for mentorship, ask for a meeting, ask to chat, affirm a recent achievement, participate in their initiative, etc.)

_____

What would be your greatest intention with this trusted advisor?

_____

_____

**Prospective trusted advisor #5:** _____

What's 1 small step you can take to deepen your relationship (e.g., send an email, ask for a coffee chat, ask for mentorship, ask for a meeting, ask to chat, affirm a recent achievement, participate in their initiative, etc.)

_____

What would be your greatest intention with this trusted advisor?

_____

_____

## Culture Changers Who Have Contributed to Your Growth

It's also important to reflect on who in your village, in the past or present, has already contributed to shaping you into a culture changer. Who are those individuals who have contributed to who you are today in positive ways? You might consider continuing to cultivate your personal and professional relationships with those individuals as well. Doing this exercise can also help you identify what you might be looking for in future trusted advisors.

Below, please list up to 5 culture changers who have contributed to your values, strengths, growth, or areas of expertise, how they contributed to your development, and what about them allowed them to contribute to your development.

*Example:*

***Culture Changer #1:*** *Janice Doe*

*How did this culture changer contribute to your values, strengths, growth, or areas of expertise?*

*Janice helped me to understand the importance of effectively managing complex relationships.*

*What was it about this culture changer that allowed them to contribute to your development?*

*Janice was as passionate about her direct report's success as she was about her own success. She would spend time regularly within our 1:1s, sharing feedback with me to help me thrive as a manager and a leader. She was a true mentor.*

**Culture Changer #1:** _____

How did this culture changer contribute to your values, strengths, growth, or areas of expertise?

_____

_____

_____

_____

What was it about this culture changer that allowed them to contribute to your development?

_____

_____

_____

_____

**Culture Changer #2:** _____

How did this culture changer contribute to your values, strengths, growth, or areas of expertise?

_____

_____

_____

_____

What was it about this culture changer that allowed them to contribute to your development?

_____

_____

_____

_____

**Culture Changer #3:** _____

How did this culture changer contribute to your values, strengths, growth, or areas of expertise?

_____

_____

_____

_____

What was it about this culture changer that allowed them to contribute to your development?

_____

_____

_____

_____

**Culture Changer #4:** _____

How did this culture changer contribute to your values, strengths, growth, or areas of expertise?

_____

_____

_____

_____

What was it about this culture changer that allowed them to contribute to your development?

_____

_____

_____

_____

**Culture Changer #5:** _____

How did this culture changer contribute to your values, strengths, growth, or areas of expertise?

_____

_____

_____

_____

What was it about this culture changer that allowed them to contribute to your development?

_____

_____

_____

_____

Which of the above culture changers, if any, might you want to be a part of your current village of advisors?

_____

_____

## Creating your Visibility Strategy

To be a culture changer, others need to know your work and your impact. You can choose to be intentional around sharing who you are and the impact you create by thinking about what key platforms you might use to enhance your influence and impact.

Reflect on and list 5 platforms that you should utilize to enhance your influence and impact. Examples of platforms include 1:1 check-ins with your manager, team meetings, LinkedIn, weekly networking events, media recognition, and more.

*Example:*

**Platform:** LinkedIn

One way I will use this platform to increase my visibility over the next 60 days:

I will connect with all of my current and previous colleagues on LinkedIn after updating my profile.

**Platform # 1:** _____

One way I will use this platform to increase my visibility over the next 60 days:

_____

**Platform # 2:** _____

One way I will use this platform to increase my visibility over the next 60 days:

_____

**Platform # 3:** _____

One way I will use this platform to increase my visibility over the next 60 days:

_____

**Platform # 4:** _____

One way I will use this platform to increase my visibility over the next 60 days:

_____

**Platform # 5:** _____

One way I will use this platform to increase my visibility over the next 60 days:

_____


## Your Culture Changer Vision Statement

Think about how you desire to create more influence and impact professionally and personally. You'll be writing a vision statement below about what kind of culture changer you'd like to be. Reflect on the values that drive you and the inspiration behind them.

My culture changer vision statement:

_Example:_

_My vision is to utilize my problem-solving, ability to connect deeply with others, and logistics management skills to create and launch informal and formal initiatives that greatly impact the results and culture of the teams and organizations that I work for._

_____

_____

_____

_____

What top 3 ongoing behaviors or action steps will allow you to attain your vision?

_Example:_
_1. Taking initiative to confidently and collaboratively solve problems on teams._
_2. Connecting informally and formally 1:1 with team members within and beyond my team on a weekly basis._
_3. Consistently ensuring that the right quality control measures are in place to ensure success for projects._

1. _____

2. _____

3. _____

## From Ripples to Waves: Sustaining Forward Movement

**Your 90-day, 6-month, and 1-year plan:** Being a culture changer comes as a result of an ongoing commitment to increase your influence and impact in positive ways. Create a 90-day, 6-month, and 1-year plan for how you will do this. Include touchpoints with key stakeholders, platforms you'll be using for visibility, and top behaviors you'll be striving to implement along the way. Definitely be sure to also include monthly or quarterly time to reflect on your accomplishments, any desired shifts to your plan, and whether your next priorities should shift.

Know that "becoming the ripple" and being a culture changer are synonymous. Being laser-focused on consistently expanding your influence in positive ways allows you to have a greater impact on your life, your role, your company, and society as a whole.

When you align with the greatest version of who you're meant to be, the result is a legacy and impact beyond what you could imagine.

# Reflections

_____

_____

_____

_____

_____

_____

_____

_____

_____

_____

_____

_____

_____

_____

_____

_____

_____

_____

# CHAPTER 11
# Implement the "One-thing" Principle

*"Someone's sitting in the shade
today because someone planted
a tree a long time ago."*

**—WARREN BUFFETT**

If you're reading this, most likely you're an individual who has been working diligently to be successful and is someone who also puts significant work into making sure that others around you are doing well. You've also most likely experienced what it feels like to be overwhelmed or burnt out trying to do all that you feel you must do. This "one thing" principle enables you to focus on the most important things that could shift your results in your professional life. For example, if you're a manager, "one thing" that might most shift your results is having regularly occurring status meetings with your staff. Or if you're a sales leader, "one thing" that might most shift your results is shifting the time you spend on administrative work to your afternoons when your energy might be down, while shifting key sales calls to your most energized time of the day. Complete the exercise below to hone in on what your "one thing" might be.

## Identifying your "One Thing"

First, we'll repeat an exercise from Chapter 6. You can either do this over again based on whether your priorities at work have changed, or simply transfer your top 3 most important activities or priorities associated with each bucket below, and skip ahead to section d. below.

1. **Reflect on your buckets.** Think of all of the different components of your professional work (For example: strategy, operations, stakeholder management, etc.).

   a. **Identify your 3 main buckets.** If you had to split your work into just 3 buckets, considering what your most important work is, what would those be? Write down those 3 buckets in the table below.

   b. **Draft your priorities.** Then write your 5 - 10 most important activities or priorities associated with each of those buckets in the table below.

   c. **Identify your top priorities in each bucket.** Circle your top 3 most important activities or priorities associated with each bucket. You should have 9 top activities or priorities circled.

   d. **Identify your number one priority in each bucket.** Place a star next to your number 1 priority associated with each bucket. You should have 3 top activities or priorities starred.

   e. **Identify your number 1 priority overall.** Place a rectangle around your number 1 current priority overall out of all of your top current priorities.

*Example:*

---

*Professional Work Bucket 1:*

*Stakeholder Management*

---

*5 - 10 Most Important Activities or Priorities Associated With This Bucket:*

*1. Sending status updates to board members quarterly*

*2. Drafting and sending letters to investors*

*3. Reaching out to do project status checks with key vendors*

*4. Revising team member project plans based on stakeholder knowledge*

*\*5. Meeting with key stakeholders regularly*

*6. _____*

*7. _____*

---

8. _____

9. _____

10. _____

| Professional Work Bucket 1: _____ | Professional Work Bucket 2: _____ | Professional Work Bucket 3: _____ |
|---|---|---|
| 5 - 10 Most Important Activities or Priorities Associated With This Bucket: | 5 - 10 Most Important Activities or Priorities Associated With This Bucket: | 5 - 10 Most Important Activities or Priorities Associated With This Bucket: |
| 1._____ | 1._____ | 1._____ |
| 2._____ | 2._____ | 2._____ |
| 3._____ | 3._____ | 3._____ |
| 4._____ | 4._____ | 4._____ |
| 5._____ | 5._____ | 5._____ |
| 6._____ | 6._____ | 6._____ |
| 7._____ | 7._____ | 7._____ |
| 8._____ | 8._____ | 8._____ |
| 9._____ | 9._____ | 9._____ |
| 10._____ | 10._____ | 10._____ |

2.  **Exploring the impact.** Although you have several priorities, keeping the most impactful one at the center of your focus is critically important. What would the impact be if you could focus on your top professional priority with excellence? What ripple effect might be caused for you and others around you if you were able to achieve that regularly?

*Example:*
*If I could meet with key clients regularly, our repeat customer rate would drastically increase, resulting in massive revenue growth for our company. If I could meet with board members 1:1 more regularly, it could make our corporate board meetings even more efficient and aligned when it comes to the vision for our company. Meeting with our vendors regularly would also create greater alignment and decrease the time necessary for project completion.*

_____

_____

_____

_____

_____

## Aligning Your "One Thing" with Company Leadership and Culture

Part of growing your influence and impact is aligning your top activities and priorities with what matters most to your manager and the organization you work for. Being able to enhance your brand when it comes to your manager and organization can open up doors to new opportunities, result in a promotion, or even allow you to advocate more for yourself, those around you, or your customers.

How does your "one thing" currently align with your manager's goals and priorities? What adjustments, or enhancements, if any, should you make to your "one thing" to better align it with your company leadership's goals or your company culture?

*Example:*
*My manager would want to ensure he's in the loop about any critical conversations I'm having with key stakeholders, and he may actually desire to meet with certain key stakeholders that I might usually meet with. Adjusting my "one thing" might look like me reflecting more on which key stakeholders may be best for my manager to meet with, and coordinating those meetings for my manager in order for him to meet the objectives for his role as well.*

_____

_____

_____

## Planning for Implementation and Impact

What's exciting about your "one thing" is the prospective impact it can make for you and those around you—a true ripple effect. Your "one thing" in your role as an HR executive might be to hire a top-performing training and development team. Or maybe your "one thing" as a marketing leader is to double engagement on your next campaign. As a franchise owner, maybe your "one thing" is to support your sales team in hitting their sales goals this quarter. Or as an operations executive, your "one thing" could be to reduce the time taken to implement specific production processes for your team by at least 10%. We know that the results of any of the above initiatives could shift the trajectory of a team or organization and position leaders to be culture changers within their organization. Still, we also know that this kind of laser focus on "one thing" requires planning for implementation and impact.

What can you do over the next 30 days, 60 days, 90 days, and 6 months, to accomplish your "one thing," and what might the impact be over each timeframe?

| Timeframe | Action Steps | Prospective Impact |
|---|---|---|
| **30 days** | *Example: Identify key stakeholders who are essential to meet with regularly along with identifying a specific meeting cadence for each key stakeholder. Identify the right system to remind me that those meetings should be scheduled and that tracks when they are scheduled.* | *Example: This can create clarity around key stakeholders I would be focusing on meeting with regularly and establish a clear system for outreach.* |
| **60 days** | *Example: Based on key stakeholder feedback, complete a key stakeholder meeting audit. What's going well with key stakeholder meetings, what could be better, and how can meeting content, structure, and other associated logistics be adjusted?* | *Example: This can create more clarity around what is already working and what can be shifted for the most results-driven plan to be created.* |

| 90 days | | |
|---|---|---|
| | *Example: Implement a new key stakeholder meeting approach and key stakeholder meeting tracking system to facilitate regularly occurring meetings with key stakeholders.* | *Example: This can drastically increase key stakeholder trust, engagement, sales, and collaboration.* |
| 6 months | *Example: Assess meeting cadences, lengths, content, and results and tweak as needed.* | *Example: This ensures that this system of meeting with key stakeholders regularly is being assessed well.* |

One year from now, what would the greatest impacts be of you implementing your "one thing"?

*Example:*
*The greatest impacts of implementing my "one thing" could be increased revenue, engagement, and results from our key stakeholders, along with an enhanced brand associated with my department and my role.*

_____

_____

_____

## From Ripples to Waves: Sustaining Forward Movement

**Reflecting on your progress:** When it comes to "becoming the ripple," sometimes less is more. Having "one thing" that guides your focus allows you to hone in on what's most important in a world where there are so many competing priorities, both personally and professionally. In order to ensure that you're on track with making progress on your "one thing," schedule a check in with yourself every 30 days to identify what progress you've made with your "one thing", what you've learned is most effective when it comes to implementing your "one thing", and where you feel you may want to shift your approach to implementing your "one thing".

Your ability to consistently hone your approach to your "one thing" allows you to be positioned as a culture changer within your company who knows how to create transformative change and who takes action to push change forward thoughtfully and consistently.

Let your "one thing" be
your North Star that guides
your strategic action towards
the greatest results.

# Reflections

_____

_____

_____

_____

_____

_____

_____

_____

_____

_____

_____

_____

_____

_____

_____

_____

_____

_____

_____

_____

# CHAPTER 12

# Be the Change You Want to See

*"When we strive to become better than we are, everything around us becomes better too."*

**—PAULO COELHO**

Since launching my consulting firm, I have personally facilitated individual, group, and team coaching for over 3600 hours for more than ten years. As I was receiving coaching training to become a certified coach, one thing that I learned is that your thoughts turn into your feelings, and those feelings turn into your actions.

Thoughts → Feelings → Actions

Here are 2 examples of this:

**EXAMPLE 1:**

**Thoughts** = Your manager communicates to you that she is assigning you to lead a big project. You may be thinking about how you have too much work on your plate already.

**Feelings** = You thinking about having too much work already might lead you to feel resentment and overwhelm.

**Actions** = Your feelings of overwhelm and resentment might result in you not communicating well with your manager throughout the duration of that big project.

**EXAMPLE 2:**

**Thoughts** = Your manager communicates to you that she is assigning you to lead a big project. You may be thinking that this project could be the perfect opportunity to gain more visibility and potentially secure a promotion, either internally at your current company or another organization.

**Feelings** = That thought may lead you to feel grateful for the opportunity, but curious as to how you'll balance it with your other responsibilities. You might also feel more confident in your capabilities as a result of being chosen for this big project.

**Actions** = You might use your feelings of gratitude, curiosity, and confidence to advocate very professionally for what work might be reduced for you to focus on the big project. You might also ensure you're communicating regularly with your manager to ensure they have visibility into all that you're accomplishing when it comes to key milestones for your project.

## Exploring your Past Approaches to Challenging Circumstances

Think about 3 experiences over the past 3 - 6 months where you don't feel you responded in alignment with your values or you didn't respond as the best version of yourself? Write below what you feel your thoughts, feelings, and actions were in those experiences:

*Example:*

*Experience 1 Brief Description: Responding to my manager's pushback*

*Thoughts = I felt my manager should have gone with the idea I shared in our team meeting.*

*Feelings = I felt disappointed and insignificant.*

*Actions = My answers in the meeting came off as frustrated and short.*

**Experience 1 Brief Description:** _____

Thoughts = _____

Feelings = _____

Actions = _____

**Experience 2 Brief Description:** _____

Thoughts = _____

Feelings = _____

Actions = _____


**Experience 3 Brief Description:** _____

Thoughts = _____

Feelings = _____

Actions = _____


Overall, what approach in the past do you think you took that didn't work as well for you? You can write, for example, "I notice that when [overall or specific kind of experience] happens, I sometimes have [action I took], because [explanation for why you think this has happened]."

*Example:*
*I notice that when I feel that others are disrespecting me, it can cause me not to present the best version of myself, even if they may not be trying to be disrespectful to me. This may happen because I feel that person is attacking me personally, rather than feeling like they are sharing a perspective or feeling from their frame of reference about a problem.*

_____

_____

_____


## Defining New Approaches to Challenging Circumstances

As you are in the process of "becoming the ripple," you will continue to realize that there are always opportunities to shift more into who you desire to be. Think about your 3 experiences that you referenced above where you don't feel you responded in alignment with your values, or you didn't respond as the best version of yourself. Write below what you feel your new thoughts, feelings, and actions could be in those moments in the future if you're aligning with your values or thinking, feeling, and acting in alignment with what it means to be your best self. You can also identify other experiences below and how you want to respond in those circumstances:

*Past or Prospective Experience #1 Brief Description:* <u>Responding to my manager's pushback</u>

*Desired Thoughts =* <u>My manager is providing feedback or direction on the idea and not on my character or capabilities.</u>

*Desired Feelings =* <u>I desire to feel appreciation and curiosity about the advantages and disadvantages of his perspective.</u>

*Desired Actions =* <u>I desire to work as a collaborative partner with my manager to help our team have the best outcome.</u>

**Past or Prospective Experience #1 Brief Description:** _____

Desired Thoughts = _____

Desired Feelings = _____

Desired Actions = _____

**Past or Prospective Experience #2 Brief Description:** _____

Desired Thoughts = _____

Desired Feelings = _____

Desired Actions = _____

**Past or Prospective Experience #3 Brief Description:** _____

Desired Thoughts = _____

Desired Feelings = _____

Desired Actions = _____

Overall, what approach in the future would work well for you? You can write, for example, "In the future, when [overall or specific kind of experience] happens, I desire to believe [desired thoughts] and feel [desired feelings] so that I can [action I want to take], because [explanation for why you think this is important]."

*Example:*
*In the future, when people's responses or comments don't align with my values or perspectives, I desire to believe they are presenting a perspective, and feel curious so that I can utilize my problem-solving skills to identify what to do*

*or say next. I think this is important because it allows me to remain calm and focused, which can lead to a better outcome.*

_____

_____

_____

## A Visual Reminder of Your 3 Approaches

Where can you place a reminder or even a visual that helps you remember how you'd like to approach different situations when it comes to what you think, feel, and do?

*Example:*
*In a daily calendar reminder*

_____

_____

## Understanding Your Triggers

What are 3 triggers or circumstances that cause you to sometimes think, feel, and act in a way that doesn't align with who you desire to be? What would your old response have been to that trigger, and what is your plan for having a better response in the future?

*Example:*

*Trigger #1: Getting pushback from my manager about an idea*

*Your old response: Feeling defensive and providing only brief, short responses as a result*

*Your new plan: Remind myself of who I'm striving to be with a short affirmation in the moment during the conversation*

**Trigger #1:** _____

Your old response: _____

Your new plan: _____

**Trigger #2:** _____

Your old response: _____

Your new plan: _____


**Trigger #3:** _____

Your old response: _____

Your new plan: _____


## A Letter to Your Future Self

Imagine your future self 10 years from today, who has strived to embody the new approaches you shared in the previous exercise and is consistently working on continuously becoming a ripple, both professionally and personally. Reflect on what you might think, feel, and do as a result of those new approaches. Write yourself a letter now to that future version of yourself 10 years from today. You can share gratitude, encouragement, what you foresee might be happening in your life at that time after embodying your new approaches regularly, or anything you feel led to write about.

_Example:_

_Dear future self,_

_Thank you for all that you have done over these past 10 years to strive to embody your best self. I know it hasn't been easy, but I genuinely appreciate you._

_These days, you've been working on thinking more about the positive intent others might have in any situation, trying to see every challenge as a problem to solve, or finding things to be grateful for in the midst of those challenges._

_You've been striving to feel more gratitude, appreciation, calm, and curiosity, not only in challenging times but in good times as well._

_As a result, you are taking actions that align with being the best version of yourself, fostering stronger connections with others, collaborating more effectively, and achieving tangible results from your efforts._

_Continue to do all that you know is going to get you closer to where you know you can, should, and will be. You already see what you've been able to accomplish, even amid your challenges, and your possibilities continue to be endless!_

_Love,_

_Your past self (AKA your biggest fan)_

_____

_____

_____

_____

_____

_____

_____

_____

_____

_____

_____

## From Ripples to Waves: Sustaining Forward Movement

**Weekly accountability and reflection:** If there's one thing you can take away from the exercises above, it's that no matter what you have done or who you have been in the past, you always have the opportunity to embody more of who you aspire to be. One way to work on this and sustain forward movement is to schedule time weekly for accountability and reflection. During this scheduled reflection time, you can journal about what you did that week that reflects your new approaches, where you reverted to your past approaches and why, and what your vision is for your week ahead.

As you learn from the past and strive to be more of who you desire to be in the future, you can use the exercises in this chapter to continuously embody what it means to be "becoming the ripple" personally and professionally.

Being more of who you aspire
to be over time can create a
ripple effect for you and those
around you in ways beyond
what you could imagine.

# Reflections

# PART 5

# YOUR SPECIAL TOUCH

# CHAPTER 13

# Identify Your Special Sauce

*"We are what we repeatedly do.
Excellence, then, is not an act, but a habit."*

**—ARISTOTLE**

What if you knew for sure what unique gifts and talents could allow you to increase your influence and impact? Every one of us has a special combination of who we are that makes us each unique. It's like a special recipe that comes as a result of our own experiences, background, influences, and stories. It's your special sauce.

## Reflecting on Your Special Sauce

The following exercise will help you reflect on how your special sauce has recently appeared in your work.

Over the past 3 months, what are moments or projects when you've felt most energized and confident in your work? What strengths did you utilize in those moments or projects?

*Example:*
*Some of the moments over the past 3 months when I felt most energized and confident in my work were when I was talking to key stakeholders internally and externally within our company to gain insights towards drafting our strategic plan, and also when I was pitching our new strategic plan to our team and received positive feedback. I*

*utilized my strengths in being able to connect deeply with others, being able to synthesize large pieces of information, and being able to present in an engaging way in those examples.*

_____

_____

_____

_____

_____

_____

Some of our Special Sauce may have been evident since childhood. What gifts, talents, or positive approaches to life or work have been present for you since childhood?

*Example:*
*Since childhood, I've been someone who has loved to see everyone around me do well and have had the ability to connect deeply with those around me. I've also been someone who strove for excellence and loved to serve since being a child.*

_____

_____

_____

## Special Sauce Survey

Create a short survey that you will use with 3 colleagues, 3 friends, and 3 family members to further explore what your special sauce might be. Then document your answers as you explore your special sauce.

What will the 3 questions be on your survey for your colleagues, friends, and family? Some examples of questions are:

1.  What do you believe are my top 3 strengths?
2.  What do I exude when I am at my best?
3.  What do you think I do more naturally than others?

Please write your 3 brief questions for your mini survey, along with notes from answers from 3 colleagues, 3 friends, and 3 family members below. You can ask the questions to respondents verbally or in writing:

*Example:*

*Mini survey question:*

<u>*What do you believe are my top 3 strengths?*</u>

*Mini survey question #1 responses notes:*

<u>*Your ability to lead. Your ability to create a vision. You are always ready to take action on anything you dream of. You're one of the kindest people I know. You help others to be confident. You really are changing the world. You are a changemaker. You are so inspiring.*</u>

Mini survey question # 1:

_____

Mini survey question #1 responses notes:

_____

_____

_____

_____

_____

Mini survey question # 2:

_____

Mini survey question #2 responses notes:

_____

_____

_____

_____

_____

_____

Mini survey question # 3:

_____

Mini survey question #3 responses notes:

_____

_____

_____

_____

_____

Highlight responses that were very similar across all 3 survey questions in the same color. You can use different highlighter colors for different kinds of responses. For example, you might highlight all answers that are associated with you being compassionate with an orange color. Reflect on the trends that you observe in the responses. You can also use an online word cloud tool to create a word cloud with the words that stood out from responses.

## Your Top 3 Ingredients

Your strengths are part of what makes you so unique and are an essential part of your special sauce. Your special sauce should be the foundation for the kind of ripple effect you hope to have on the world, as you are "becoming the ripple." Your special sauce may relate to the 3 keys you explored earlier in this workbook that you exude when you're at your best. When you know what makes you so unique and valuable, it allows you to no longer compete with others so much as you are striving to be the very best version of yourself, exploring what excellence looks like specifically for you. Based on the previous exercises, how would you describe the top 3 ingredients of your special sauce? Based on the earlier exercises, how would you describe the top 3 ingredients that embody your special sauce?

*Example:*

***Write 1 word or phrase to describe 1 of your top strengths:*** *Visionary*

*Share more about this strength as it relates to you:*

*I have the ability to create an idea, develop an action plan for it, and mobilize others around that idea.*

*Write 1 or more examples of when you've implemented this strength:*

*I created and led initiatives in multiple organizations that I worked for, which were the vision of my manager or my vision, with successful outcomes in each case.*

**1. Write 1 word or phrase to describe 1 of your top strengths:** _____

Share more about this strength as it relates to you:

_____

_____

_____

Write 1 or more examples of when you've implemented this strength:

_____

_____

_____

**2. Write 1 word or phrase to describe 1 of your top strengths:** _____

Share more about this strength as it relates to you:

_____

_____

_____

Write 1 or more examples of when you've implemented this strength:

_____

_____

**3. Write 1 word or phrase to describe 1 of your top strengths:** _____

Share more about this strength as it relates to you:

_____

_____

_____

Write 1 or more examples of when you've implemented this strength:

_____

_____

_____

## Daily Strengths Practice Plan

In the table below, write 3 ways you can practice each strength weekly, along with 1 stretch goal to enhance how you apply this strength in the next 30 days:

| Strength | 3 Ways to Practice This Strength Weekly | 30-Day Stretch Goal to Apply This Strength |
|---|---|---|
| | 1.<br><br>2.<br><br>3. | |
| *Example:*<br>*Visionary* | *Example:*<br>*1. Take on projects that require creativity and problem-solving*<br>*2. Initiate or contribute to action plans for projects*<br>*3. Support others in creating or expanding their vision* | *Example:*<br>*Create a new or expanded vision for a project I'm working on and share that vision.* |

|  | 1. | |
|  | 2. | |
|  | 3. | |
|  | 1. | |
|  | 2. | |
|  | 3. | |

What are 1 - 3 ways that you will remember to implement the plan above?

*Example:*

*I will use sticky notes, phone reminders, and affirmations posted on a flip chart to remember to implement the plan above.*

_____

_____

_____

## Your Special Sauce Statement

Write a 2-3 sentence statement that embodies your unique strengths and gifts.

*Example*
*My special sauce is igniting confidence, clarity, and connection in others through strategic insight, authentic communication, and a deep belief in people's potential. Whether I'm coaching a leader, facilitating a team breakthrough, or speaking to hundreds of individuals, I bring warmth, resourcefulness, and results-driven intention that empowers others to rise with purpose and impact.*

_____

_____

_____

_____

_____

_____

## From Ripples to Waves: Sustaining Forward Movement

**Create a strengths-in-action log:** Exploring your special sauce can be a truly valuable, eye-opening experience because it forces you to look at yourself, your potential, and your value through other people's eyes. It's not about ignoring the challenging things you've experienced in life or at work. But rather, when you can take what you have experienced–both good and bad–and use it towards embodying characteristics or values that make you a more effective leader, even those challenging experiences can contribute well to your special sauce.

One way to sustain forward movement when it comes to your special sauce is to create a strengths-in-action log. In a physical journal or digital document, you can write daily for a 3-day or 7-day span about 1 moment each day when you intentionally used 1 aspect of your special sauce. Tracking this consistently allows you to be even more intentional about looking for ways to apply your special sauce in various circumstances.

Remember to not only embrace your special sauce and acknowledge its value, but also to hone it regularly to grow your influence and impact through the ripples it creates.

Discovering your special sauce is a gift. Implementing your special sauce is a gift to the world and the foundation for your impact.

# Reflections

# CHAPTER 14

# Infuse Your Strengths Into Your Work

*"Be sure you put your feet in the right place, then stand firm."*

**—ABRAHAM LINCOLN**

We can also refer to your special sauce as your special touch. Infusing your special touch into your work might allow you to feel more fulfilled and impactful at work. It can have a direct correlation to the ripple effect you can have on those around you professionally. The following chapter guides you in how you can practically integrate your special touch into various aspects of your work on an ongoing basis. As you incorporate your gifts, talents, and strengths into your work, you are steadily infusing more of your influence and impact into your work, creating a significant ripple effect.

## Strengths Mapping

On the visual map below of your work ecosystem, write about where your strengths are being utilized well or underused.

Components of your work ecosystem often depend on your role, but some prospective aspects of your ecosystem that you can explore might include:

| With colleagues | With managers | On teams within projects | In onboarding | In training |
| --- | --- | --- | --- | --- |

| Within daily tasks | In work committees | At work events | For special projects | For operations |
|---|---|---|---|---|
| For suggestions | For feedback | To mentor | For new initiatives | In conflict |

*Example*:

*Aspect of your ecosystem:*

*With my manager*

*How well are your strengths being utilized in this aspect of your work?*

*My strengths are being utilized fairly well, but I do not feel I am sharing my strengths enough with my manager.*

| Aspect of your ecosystem: | Aspect of your ecosystem: | Aspect of your ecosystem: |
|---|---|---|
| How well are your strengths being utilized in this aspect of your work? | How well are your strengths being utilized in this aspect of your work? | How well are your strengths being utilized in this aspect of your work? |

| Aspect of your ecosystem: | Aspect of your ecosystem: | Aspect of your ecosystem: |
|---|---|---|
| _____ | _____ | _____ |
| How well are your strengths being utilized in this aspect of your work? | How well are your strengths being utilized in this aspect of your work? | How well are your strengths being utilized in this aspect of your work? |
| _____ _____ _____ | _____ _____ _____ | _____ _____ _____ |
| Aspect of your ecosystem: | Aspect of your ecosystem: | Aspect of your ecosystem: |
| _____ | _____ | _____ |
| How well are your strengths being utilized in this aspect of your work? | How well are your strengths being utilized in this aspect of your work? | How well are your strengths being utilized in this aspect of your work? |
| _____ _____ _____ | _____ _____ _____ | _____ _____ _____ |

## Special Touch Opportunity Inventory

What are 5 professional spaces or tasks where you can be showing up more with aspects of your special touch? Some examples are in team meetings, in client calls, when attaining a new project, etc. How can you show up more with your special touch in that location or for that task in a way that is practical and measurable?

*Example:*

*1. Professional space or task:* <u>With my manager</u>

*How can you utilize more of your special touch in this location or when engaging in this task?*

*I can ensure I'm integrating strengths that I usually might not incorporate into a project to share my capabilities more with my manager.*

*When will you start implementing this approach?*

*Tomorrow*

**1. Professional space or task:** _____

How can you utilize more of your special touch in this location or when engaging in this task?

_____

_____

When will you start implementing this approach? _____

**2. Professional space or task:** _____

How can you utilize more of your special touch in this location or when engaging in this task?

_____

_____

When will you start implementing this approach? _____

**3. Professional space or task:** _____

How can you utilize more of your special touch in this location or when engaging in this task?

_____

_____

When will you start implementing this approach? _____

**4. Professional space or task:** _____

How can you utilize more of your special touch in this location or when engaging in this task?

_____

_____

When will you start implementing this approach? _____

**5. Professional space or task:** _____

How can you utilize more of your special touch in this location or when engaging in this task?

_____

_____

When will you start implementing this approach? _____

## Special Touch Integration Calendar

What are 3 - 5 upcoming events, like 1:1s, meetings, or other events, where you can intentionally implement 1 element of your special touch? What would success look like for you at each event when it comes to integrating your special touch?

*Example:*

**Event** *1:1 Meeting with My Manager*                    *Date 9/12*

*What does success look like when it comes to integrating your special sauce at this event?*

*As I'm updating my manager on the status of projects, I'll share what I've been proactive about doing that also integrates my strengths.*

**Event #1** _____          Date_____

What does success look like when it comes to integrating your special sauce at this event?

_____

_____

**Event #2** _____          Date_____

What does success look like when it comes to integrating your special sauce at this event?

_____

_____

**Event #3** _____ Date_____

What does success look like when it comes to integrating your special sauce at this event?

_____

_____

**Event #4** _____ Date_____

What does success look like when it comes to integrating your special sauce at this event?

_____

_____

**Event #5** _____ Date_____

What does success look like when it comes to integrating your special sauce at this event?

_____

_____

## Creating a Daily Special Touch Reflection Prompt

Many individuals who you might perceive as successful had created ways to be intentional about how they showed up on a regular basis when it came to their professional or personal pursuits. What can you tell yourself daily at the beginning of your work day and the end of your work day to remind you to infuse your special touch into your work?

Before-work (or morning) statement or question(s) about your strengths

Example:
_Today, I will commit to being inspiring, energizing, and a guide in service to myself and in service to others._

_____

_____

After-work (or evening) statement or question(s) about your strengths

*Example:*
*Where did I have a chance to use my special touch today? What am I proud of today when it comes to my special touch? What do I want to shift when it comes to my special touch?"*

_____

_____

Keep in mind that each ripple you create regarding your impact should have your special touch infused through it, as you are "becoming the ripple." You or even your colleagues might notice more and more of a shift in how you show up as you take your gifts, talents, and strengths to the next level at work over time. Most importantly, you will grow your influence and impact towards the success that you desire over time. Remember, from the stories that I shared earlier, your possibilities are truly endless.

## Integrating a Feedback Loop

Utilize a trusted colleague, advisor, coach, mentor, or colleague to help you operate more consistently with your special touch. Share your special touch with them and invite them to offer feedback on how much they observe you aligning with your special touch, and where you might need to shift.

Which trusted colleague(s), advisor(s), coach(es), mentor(s), or colleague(s) might you use to do this?

*Example:*
*My mentor at work, Jane Doe.*

_____

## From Ripples to Waves: Sustaining Forward Movement

**Monthly strengths check-in:** After integrating your special touch into your everyday work and life, it can be valuable to journal where you are and where you'd like to be when it comes to utilizing your unique strengths more daily. Try journaling the answers to the following questions after 30 days of using your special touch more consistently:

- Which strength am I using most?
- What has surprised me when it comes to how I'm using my strengths?

- What were some of the most prominent results of my consistently using my strengths?
- What is a shift I'd like to make in how I'm using my strengths moving forward?

My hope is that, even before you begin journaling, you'll start to feel and see the impact of adding your special touch to the unique recipe that is your life. I hope that you get to see the ripples of impact you create *turn into waves*. The possibilities for the results of this implementation are truly endless.

Somewhere, a person, project, or company is on the verge of being greatly impacted as a result of you walking in your strengths. You are talented, capable, and ready to share those strengths with the world.

# Reflections

# CHAPTER 15

# Becoming the Ripple: Making W.A.V.E.S.™

*"Do not stop thinking of life as an adventure. You have no security unless you can live bravely, excitingly, imaginatively; unless you can choose a challenge instead of competence."*

**—ELEANOR ROOSEVELT**

As we recap previous chapters of this workbook, you'll explore the W.A.V.E.S. acronym that was used throughout this workbook to describe how you increase your influence and impact personally and professionally in order to be "becoming the ripple" for yourself and others.

As I mentioned in my book, Becoming the Ripple: Your Guide to Exponentially Increasing Your Professional Success and Influence, "Companies and organizations need individuals who will not only meet the expectations of their roles, but who understand their **w**hy, who will take strategic **a**ction, who know their **v**oice needs to be one that creates influence, who take their work **e**nvironment to the next level by what they contribute to it, and who are clear on their **s**pecial touch in a way that their strengths are infused into their work.

That kind of individual is a leader who not only creates a ripple effect of impact within their companies but is always thinking of ways to constantly be "becoming the ripple"–an active, ongoing commitment to continuously pursue growing their influence and impact wherever they go within their companies."

## Your Why: A Motivation Reflection

As you reflect on the exercises you've done throughout this workbook and reflect on your why, what do you believe drives you to do the work that you do professionally, even on the most challenging days? List 3 - 5 influences, experiences, ideas, people, or anything else that keep you motivated to do all that you do.

*Example:*
*1. My family who have come before me and their legacy.*
*2. The mentors who have paved the way for me to be who I am today and who share what they see in me.*
*3. My team members who I have been given the responsibility to influence.*
*4. Individuals who have changed the course of history based on their approach to their lives, work, and legacy.*
*5. My faith and belief that I am being used for a greater purpose at work and home.*

1. _____

2. _____

3. _____

4. _____

5. _____

How can you keep these motivations in front of you daily, or how are you already keeping those motivations in front of you daily? Some examples to consider utilizing are phone reminders, sticky notes, or an accountability partner.

*Example:*
*I will have a daily calendar reminder with my greatest motivations.*

_____

_____

_____

## Your Action: A Becoming the Ripple Action Plan

Imagine that it is a year from now, and someone shares a note with you that has a few paragraphs about the positive impact you have made in your professional role. What are a few things you believe you'd want to be stated in that note?

*Example:*
*I would want that note to highlight that I've been inspiring, been in service, have been innovative, have been a mentor to others, or have contributed to enhanced results for my team.*

_____

_____

_____

_____

_____

What are 5 specific, strategic action steps you can take over the next 90 days that would greatly impact your team, company, customers, or clients that might be connected to your previous answer? And when can you take those action steps?

*Example:*
*Establish a key stakeholder meeting cadence and strategy to further cultivate relationships with our key stakeholders.*
    *Date to complete this action step: 1/15*

1. _____

    Date to complete this action step: _____

2. _____

    Date to complete this action step: _____

3. _____

    Date to complete this action step: _____

4. _____

    Date to complete this action step: _____

5. _____

    Date to complete this action step: _____

## Your Voice: Your top 3 Opportunities

What are 3 opportunities that you have to use your voice more strategically in your role at work? Examples of this are speaking up more confidently at sales meetings, preparing and sharing more data and research at team meetings, volunteering to facilitate more difficult conversations, mastering negotiations, or sharing more bold ideas.

*Example:*
*Volunteering to facilitate more difficult conversations at work*
    *Date to complete this action step: 11/31*

1. _____

    Date to complete this action step: _____

2. _____

    Date to complete this action step: _____

3. _____

    Date to complete this action step: _____

## Your Environment: An Intentionality Audit

Think about conversations and meetings you've participated in more recently. Identify what energy you most recently have tended to bring into different physical or virtual spaces. Then, please write down what you desire for people to feel after engaging with you if you are being very intentional.

*Example:*
*I desire that after people engage with me, if I am being very intentional, they would feel inspired, energized, and supported.*

_____

_____

_____

What are 3 small shifts you can make to be more intentional about how you want people to feel after engaging with you, and when might you implement those shifts?

*Example:*
*I can ensure I'm practicing empathetic listening with others in various roles at work.*
   *Date to complete this action step: 11/31*

1. _____

   Date to complete this action step: _____

2. _____

   Date to complete this action step: _____

3. _____

   Date to complete this action step: _____

## Your Special Touch: Being More Intentional about your Special Sauce

What are your current top 3 unique strengths that embody your special sauce?

*Example:*
*1. Logistics Management*
*2. Troubleshooting*
*3. Empathetic Listening*

1. _____

2. _____

3. _____

What are 3 ways they have already contributed to your success in the past?

*Example:*
*1. I have been able to spearhead and implement operational plans as we transitioned cloud systems at work.*
*2. I have been able to utilize troubleshooting to identify prospective compliance issues that would have cost our company $1 million in additional unnecessary expenses.*
*3. I utilized empathetic listening to de-escalate an issue with one of our highest-paying customers and to come to a resolution swiftly.*

1. _____

_____

2. _____

_____

3. _____

_____

What are 3 ways you will be even more intentional about utilizing your special sauce over the next 90 days?

*Example:*
*1. I will ensure I'm proactively addressing logistics management needs for upcoming projects.*
*2. I'll be troubleshooting an upcoming project with our finance team to ensure we're preventing avoidable errors.*
*3. I will more greatly utilize empathetic listening even in meetings where I usually don't play a prominent role.*

1. _____

_____

2. _____

_____

3. _____

_____

## From Ripples to Waves: Sustaining Forward Movement

**W.A.V.E.S.™ refresher:** Your willingness to pursue creating ripples of impact personally and professionally is not only courageous and honorable, but can also be transformative, not just for you, but for your team, your company, and your loved ones. Going through this specific chapter at least annually can give you a big-picture reminder of the core of what we discussed throughout this workbook as the foundation for "becoming the ripple." Consider scheduling time annually to come back to this chapter and assess how you might be integrating the W.A.V.E.S.™ concepts mentioned in this chapter in your everyday life. 77

Remember that you are the only person in the world who has been born with the experiences, ideas, vision, and approach that you have. Operating fully in your gifts and talents to do what you're called to do, despite challenges that come your way, impacts everything around you. In the process, you are "becoming the ripple" that impacts everything around you.

If you have completed all of the exercises in this workbook as a whole, you have done a great deal of work to become the ripple that you are meant to be. Continue onwards in the pursuit of influence and impact. When people with great vision and strong values become ripples, our companies, our teams, our communities, and our world as a whole become better. So thank you for all that you are doing now and all that you'll continue to do to be "becoming the ripple" that our world needs more of.

Your obedience to shifting and changing as you grow makes an indelible mark, not only on you, but on everything around you. You can create the ripple that makes the shift that transforms you and those around you.

# Reflections

---

---

---

---

---

---

---

---

---

---

---

---

---

---

---

---

---

---

---

---

# AFTERWORD

*"You can never leave footprints that last
if you are always walking on tiptoe."*

**—LEYMAH GBOWEE**

Thank you so much for completing this workbook. After writing and publishing Becoming the Ripple: Your Guide to Exponentially Increasing Your Professional Success and Influence, a few individuals who purchased the first book asked me if I had a workbook available. This workbook is a direct result of my taking the time to create what was a need for the colleagues, leaders, and companies in my circle who asked for it. I'm excited for the impact that you might experience through it.

The topics I wrote about in this workbook were topics that organizations asked me to speak about during the height of the COVID-19 pandemic in 2020. I created the WAVES™ framework, which I reference in this workbook, in response to organizations that, during that time, wanted to have a facilitator come in to support teams with more connection, productivity, and resilience amid one of the most challenging times in history. As a result of those trainings way back then, people felt re-energized and equipped to thrive regardless of their starting place. Delivering my training sessions during that time was a powerful way that I could serve, support, and create a ripple of impact back then.

Years later, I continue to facilitate training sessions for teams and leaders across the country that include topics that I touched on in this workbook–topics that are at the core of the highest-performing teams and are aligned with the leadership values of some of the most successful companies today.

Definitely come back to the exercises in this workbook that resonate with you the most. We are all continuously "becoming the ripple," and I hope this workbook allows you to do that in the most positive way. I look forward to the impact that you'll continue to create as you continuously are "becoming the ripple" now and in the future.

Onwards and upwards,

*Daphne Valcin*

# ACKNOWLEDGMENTS

I am so grateful to Geovanni Derice, my book coach, for helping me clarify the vision and path for writing and publishing this workbook. I'm also extremely grateful for my husband, Bobby, and my children, Gabrielle and Jasmine, for their check-ins, love, and joy as I wrote this workbook. I continue to be so thankful for all of the leaders and organizations who have provided me with the opportunity to create ripples of impact for them and those around them—I'm so blessed that I get to do this work of creating and sustaining impact for others. Thanks for entrusting me to be "becoming the ripple" for you and those you serve.